# GROW YOUR RECRUITING BUSINESS

THE FIRST 3-PART BLUEPRINT TO CREATE PREDICTABLE PROFITS, RELIABLE GROWTH, AND BUSINESS FREEDOM

MIKE GIONTA

Difference Press

Washington, DC, USA



Published 2022



Cover Design: Jennifer Stimson

Editing: Trever McKenzie

# CONTENTS


*Foreword* vii

1. A Systems Approach to Recruiting 1
2. Lessons Learned in My Years of Recruiting 5
3. A Systems Approach to Recruiting 9

PART 1: CERTAIN REVENUE 13

4. Clarity of Vision 15
   Clarity of Vision Case Study 27
5. Recruiter GPS 33
   Recruiter GPS Desk-Level Case Study 43
   Recruiter GPS Firm-Level Case Study 49
6. Focused Planning 55
   Focused Planning Case Study 65

PART 2: BECOMING A PURSUED PARTNER 69

7. New Client Development 73
   New Client Development Case Study 83
8. Powerful Presentation 91
   Powerful Presentation Case Study 103
9. Flawless Execution 111
   Flawless Execution Case Study 125

PART 3: CREATING A SELF-DRIVING BUSINESS 129

10. Art of Delegation 133
    Art of Delegation Case Study 147
11. Scalable Operations 153
    Scalable Operations Case Study 163
12. Recruiter Retention 169
    Recruiter Retention Case Study 185
13. Why You Won't Implement What You Learned 189
14. Creating a Real Recruiting Business 195

*Acknowledgments* 199
*About the Author* 203
*About Difference Press* 205
*Other Books by Difference Press* 207
*Thank You* 209
*Free Resources* 211

*To my three amazing children, Meghan, Amy, and Christopher, for being my lifelong inspiration. God could not have given me better children. Thank you!*

# FOREWORD

My mom used to tell me, "When you stop learning, you start dying." Considering I was in kindergarten at the time and she was introducing the concept of death, I probably should have "learned" how to call DCF and find some foster parents. But you know what? Every year she is gone, she seems to get wiser.

When I first met Mike, he came to my seminars to learn from me. I have no idea if he learned anything, but one of the common denominators of the elite recruiters I have observed is that they speak up during the seminar and ask tough, smart questions, and they reach out after the seminar to form a relationship. Tony Robbins calls this "modeling." (Do we *really* have to have buzzwords for common sense?) I knew instantly that Mike was special. Like many successful recruiters I have met in my consulting and mentoring practice, he was an ebullient spirit. He was warm and friendly, and he was unafraid to ask pointed questions that were important to him. But unlike those same recruiters, over time, I found Mike had a listening superpower. He never spoke until the person he was speaking to was done talking.

He was self-effacing and honest. He knew he didn't know everything, and he wanted to get better. While the majority of top producers I have met have a sort of "street smarts," Mike has both a penetrating mind and a love affair with words. Recruiters want words they can use, not concepts. When you roleplay with Mike, you get pithy phrases you can use the moment you get back to your desk.

The proof of all of this is I have had Mike in my office to address my team of recruiters many times. When my partners, Pinnacle members who have heard it all, say, "That dude's legit," you know you can learn from Mike.

That brings me to Mike's book and my pet peeve about this business (okay, okay, one of my pet peeves – I have had cholic since I was three years old): "how to manage" seminars by people who have never done it. Here's how the speaking "biz" works in recruiting. First, you become a top producer. That takes years. Then, someone asks you to talk about how to run your desk, and you enjoy taking a break from the trials and tribulations of obstreperous clients and indecisive candidates to discuss your methodology. Then, two things happen. Your boss makes you a manager to (1) grow his team, and (2) keep you from getting bored and quitting. You start getting more opportunities to speak. Even though you have had practically no success managing and you find it to be more babysitting than anything else, and it drains your time on your desk. After a while, you are now getting asked, at those same conferences, to speak about "how to manage." You figure (1) "Well, I can talk about what I'm trying to do (and don't disclose billings or add in my own to fluff it up," and (2) "If all else fails, I've *been* managed for years, and I can talk about what my boss did with me." (These are always presented, ungratefully, as, "My boss is a dinosaur, and this is what's wrong with management in recruiting.")

As in sports, the top "doers" are rarely "the top coaches." You rarely find a top producer who built a big recruiting firm. By today's standards, we're talking ten to forty recruiters and five to fifteen million dollars. You can't learn how to scale from someone who doesn't meet a big payroll every Friday (with all its commensurate, sleep-depriving, anxiety-ridden, yet ultimately profoundly satisfying side effects!).

Mike did it. He can show you how to do it. He provides a system. Not "positive reinforcement" or a boost to your "emotional intelligence" – a step-by-step strategy to build your team and give you the freedom and pride and confidence you yearn for and deserve.

I read it and learned quite a lot. Somewhere, my mom is smiling.

— DANNY CAHILL, OWNER OF HOBSON ASSOCIATES AND ACCORDING TO DANNY, BESTSELLING AUTHOR AND THE RECIPIENT OF NAPS LIFETIME ACHIEVEMENT AWARD

1

# A SYSTEMS APPROACH TO RECRUITING

I see one major issue with all clients who come through The RecruiterU: the client is focusing on not losing what they have. Their focus of not failing, not sounding bad, not bothering prospects, etcetera leads to low action or, worse, *no action*. I was guilty of all of those. Those fears of "bothering," "doing it wrong," "not being good enough" almost put me out of business.

I often see recruiting firm owners who dreamt of building something substantial settle for a "bought-a-job" role as a solo operator because hiring, training, and growing is too hard and takes too much time. They also believe that once you train and develop a good recruiter, they just leave and compete with you.

Here is what I learned over the last twenty years in my business: *all* – yes, *all* – of those beliefs about getting clients, hiring recruiters, training them, and turnover *did not have to be true!*

Knowing what I know now, most recruiters were simply taught the wrong way to scale a recruiting firm using the wrong model. The model you were taught was making a million calls, taking job orders, and filling a small percent (which was still lucrative financially but weak on developing long-term clients) day after day. I don't necessarily believe that this model, when developed in the 1960s, was the wrong way. But it did not evolve.

The shift here for me, and what we teach our clients, is that revenue is no longer a mystery. Revenue is no longer held hostage by a "big biller." Revenue is a function of generating first-time interviews. *Period.* It could be as simple as me generating three first-time interviews and two other recruiters producing two each. Then, what must be true for that to happen? You can always find people to generate first-time interviews.

The concept of predictable income is unheard of in most recruiting firms. How can one predict a placement? Things blow up. Candidates and clients change their minds. We are in a business where we do not own or control *either side* of the transaction!

The first challenge for most owners I have spoken with over the past fifteen years as a coach and trainer is that they are not crystal clear on what they want out of their recruiting business. They are not clear on their role, the types of accounts they want, and their revenue.

Before they hire us to help them build their business, I ask, "How will you know our work together was a success?" Until they identify specific outcomes they are excited about, we will not take them on as a client.

Once they create a vision and a picture for what their ideal recruiting firm looks like, they do not know how to create the revenue stream in a predictable way to ensure its outcome. Uncertainty on creating consistent revenue is an area that paralyzes many in the profession as we hold ourselves accountable to *the one thing in the recruiting profession we cannot control!* Will the client make an acceptable offer, *and* will the candidate accept it?

Of course, as recruiters, we can influence this process, but we cannot control it. This area of frustration is one of the main reasons recruiters stay stuck. Mentally, they cannot directly tie their effort today into a placement that occurs four to eight weeks from now.

That is what this book is about. It is about the *systems* approach to building a recruiting firm with highly predictable outcomes. I outline the three core areas and nine key systems that, once put in place, monitored, and acted upon, will produce a seven- or multi-seven-figure recruiting firm that can run without you.

2

# LESSONS LEARNED IN MY YEARS OF RECRUITING

When I opened my recruiting firm in early 1990, I was just twenty-six years old. I had an idealistic vision to build a multi-million-dollar executive search firm with many recruiters, great clients, and a fantastic lifestyle.

I think this is what everyone aspires to – at least secretly – when they open their businesses. I wanted to build something significant – something that could ultimately run without me there. To increase the likelihood of success, I bought a franchise of Management Recruiters International (MRI); I had *no experience* in recruiting whatsoever.

I was terrible. I personally only billed about $24,000 in 1990, and my firm (with several recruiters and high turnover) billed less than $100,000. A few months into 1991, I was staring at my checking account one evening after paying bills, and I was down to my last $626. There were no receivables, and I ran through my $40,000 line of credit. With rent, recruiter draws, admin salary, loans on my furniture, and phone system, I needed $6,000 a month to stay open. Oh, and I was not, nor had I been, paying myself either.

I'll never forget that night at the office. Do I shut down and incur the approximate $150,000 in debt I accumulated to open, or do I continue?

I had one lifeline left: a $25,000 credit card line of credit at an astronomical 24 percent interest rate that I took out before I started my business in case of emergency. I realized that night that my focus for months was "not going out of business," and there I was about to go out of business! I was focused on the wrong part of the equation: the scarcity or lack side. I was focused on *not* failing versus focusing on success.

That night in May 1991, I switched focus. That $25,000 line of credit could last five or six months if I cut out some admin hours and non-productive recruiters. That night, I *decided* that I would be successful. I *decided* to go "all in" and take on more debt to make my business dream come true. I didn't know it then, but that "switch" in focus from "not failing" to "succeeding" and then taking decisive action on increasing my activity every day saved my business.

In the next couple of months, I made three placements myself, and a couple more came from my team. I only tapped into $5,000 of the high-interest debt and paid it back quickly. Success was so close all along. I just couldn't see it. I almost quit. When I *decided* to be successful, *decided* to be fully committed, and took *action,* everything changed almost immediately.

I was taught to hire seven to ten recruiters to keep one. For a time, I did hire and retain at those ratios. But like Sisyphus pushing a rock up a hill for years, I took non-exclusive contingency openings and hired recruiters who mostly quit or whom I fired.

Honestly, it sucked! I fantasized about selling my firm at

least once a month in those early years. Even though the income was okay, I was bored and highly frustrated. However, I never abandoned my decision to grow a business. As I learned in later years, when you stay committed to something and take steps and actions in alignment with that commitment, God, Spirit, and/ or the Universe *always* sends help.

For me, some of that help was Pasquale Scopelliti, my first business coach. He cold called me, and we had a great conversation. I was scared to death to hire him because he was expensive – another limiting belief. I realized if he could help me grow my business faster than I could on my own, that was an *investment* in me and my business, *not* an *expense*.

I stayed committed to growth and made the investment. In hindsight, that was the most significant investment of my life. The tens of thousands of dollars I gave him over the next decade turned into millions of dollars in revenue I would not have seen or captured on my own. Pasquale was brilliant. He saw my blind spots (there were literally hundreds) and coached me through what was false and *really true* about the opportunity in front of me.

Pasquale dragged me moaning and whining through the importance of metrics in creating predictable revenue not only at the firm level, but also at the desk level too. Initially, I hated reviewing the numbers and the meaning of those numbers with him. I wanted to talk strategy!

I remember the "a-ha" moment when I realized a million-dollar firm was only seven first-time interviews per week for a company based on our average fee and ratios. I realized that growing a recruiting firm was simply solving an algebra equation that answered the question, "What needs to be true for my business to generate seven first-time interviews per week?"

# 3

# A SYSTEMS APPROACH TO RECRUITING

This book is about the *systems* approach to building a recruiting firm with highly predictable outcomes. These systems make up the Recruiting Firm Optimizer model which outlines the nine key systems that, once put in place, monitored, and acted upon, will produce a seven- or multi-seven-figure recruiting firm that can run without you.

We begin with creating a bold vision for your future in Chapter 4. This vision is both for your recruiting and your personal life, since they are most likely intertwined. I will present to you some prompts to help you dream big.

All successful businesses have key performance indicators or metrics that are measured to help with forecasting revenue and strategizing for growth. In Chapter 5, I will outline those key metrics that every recruiting firm need to track to create predictable revenue. I will also give you the exact mathematical equation to determine your personal activity targets based upon your revenue goals.

One of the biggest challenges we hear from clients is around planning. Creating a business with predictable revenue that can run without you requires daily, weekly, quarterly, and annual planning. In Chapter 6, I will share strategies to make Focused Planning effortless so you know exactly, specifically, and precisely what you need to do each week to meet your business and revenue goals.

Your new business development or marketing must be

consistent and sufficient on a week-to-week basis. Chapter 7 will outline a few strategies you can use every week to identify people who are hiring and need you now. I will show you how to do a great diagnostic on their situation once you have someone who has an opening. You'll learn how to discover what the *real* problem is and what the *actual* consequences are for not filling it.

To elevate your client relationships, you need an excellent diagnostic process followed by a *Powerful Presentation* outlining how you will solve their problem. Positioning yourself as a trusted advisor is all about the types of questions you ask potential clients. In Chapter 8, you'll learn how to do that.

Once you agree to the excellent terms you get, it is time to walk the walk and deliver a portfolio of outstanding talent in a timely fashion. At The RecruiterU, we call that process Flawless Execution. In Chapter 9, we will show you the process of Flawless Execution.

In Chapter 10, you'll learn how to delegate effectively. The *only* path to a self-driven recruiting firm is letting go of many of the tasks and roles you are holding onto just because "no one does them as well as I do!" There is a right and wrong way to delegate. I am a recovering control freak, but once I discovered the *right* way to delegate, I became utterly addicted to it.

In Chapter 11, you'll discover why your firm must be set up to scale. Setting up to scale means creating well-defined career paths for your team members and combining them with systems in all the previous key areas of business development, client development, planning, et cetera. These are key to scaling a recruiting firm.

Finally, in Chapter 12, you'll learn about recruiter hiring and retention. It is time to rethink how you hire and retain your best recruiters. You were taught to hire raw talent that was "hungry" with potential and teach them almost everything about recruiting in their first month in the firm. What other professional service does that? Law firms? Consulting companies? Accounting firms? No. Each of those firms usually starts people in some form of "associate" role and teaches them a small entry-level part of the career with a promise of a promotion based on their ability to execute. They also have systems for attracting, hiring, and onboarding these individuals to maximize their success. They offer an opportunity for advancement instead of just "more money" as the reason to stay longer with the firm. This chapter will help you attract, hire, and retain someone who is great at helping your clients find great talent and learn how to do the same for your own business.

In all, this book will bring you through what we call the Recruiter Optimizer Model and share key lessons and strategies for each of the nine key areas. The goal is to help you create a real recruiting business that has Predictable Profits, Reliable Growth, and Business Freedom.

# PART 1: CERTAIN REVENUE

## GOING FROM ROLLERCOASTER REVENUE TO PREDICTABLE INCOME!

4

# CLARITY OF VISION

The first step of creating a *real* recruiting business is Clarity of Vision. When a new client enters one of our programs, we always start with defining their vision. A clearly defined vision is rooted in the past while addressing the present and looking toward the future. It is essential to all successful businesses. Your vision defines what you are focusing on and why those key areas are essential to your recruiting practice's success and growth. Without a clear, written vision, you will never know if you are on track to meet your goals. As a recruiting firm owner with teams, your vision will define who you are as a leader.

When I began coaching recruiting firm owners in 2007, my biggest mistake was assuming my clients knew what they wanted and what was missing from their businesses. I assumed that they understood their barriers to gaining and achieving what they desired in their lives. I also assumed that it was merely a lack of strategies and tactics that held them back from realizing their business goals. Essentially, I was working under the premise that all recruiting firm owners had a clear vision for their future, both personally and professionally.

Since I was working off my assumptions in 2007, I began the coaching process with strategies and tactics. I trained my clients on how to get a retainer, find new clients, and hire and onboard recruiters. We had a group of clients who did exceptionally well with those ideas, and we had a group of clients who did almost nothing with those ideas. These two groups were in the same or similar coaching groups. The challenge was determining the difference between the two groups.

When I reviewed my coaching notes, I discovered that the people in the group who excelled had a clear or clearer idea of where they wanted to be two, three, four, or five years out in their business and personal lives. They also had a keen understanding of how implementing the strategies I was teaching would affect their livelihoods, their roles, and the quality of their clients.

Having a clearly defined vision is essential because it becomes a litmus test for you. Many recruiters show up in the morning, attack their emails, jump on LinkedIn, and then set up a fantasy baseball or football roster. From there, they go back to checking emails, and they may make a call to pre-close a candidate on an offer. Another group of recruiters will show up each day with a predetermined plan for the week aligned with exactly where they want to be a year from now or two years from now.

A clear, written vision is what separates these two groups of recruiters. My gut feeling is that you are in that former group. When you do not have a vision, you are drifting day to day.

There is a second litmus test: If I asked you to look out a year from now, do you know where you want to be personally and professionally? What would make you tremendously happy with your progress? Most people, when asked that question, take a long time to answer it. If that is you, then you know you probably need a vision. In the absence of a vision, you will drift.

## THE PROBLEM WITH NOT HAVING A VISION

Besides aimlessly drifting from day to day, people who lack vision are bored or frustrated in their lives. I have even had clients and colleagues say that they have lost the joy in their businesses. The reason they got into the business was to not only make money but also to have fun doing it. If this feeling of boredom, frustration, or loss of joy resonates with you, ask yourself what needs to be true for you to be completely thrilled with your role in your business.

Many recruiters, especially tenured ones, drift from one day to the next with no defined plan or purpose and then get frustrated because they are not making progress. It is like a large sailing yacht leaving port, simply following the wind, rudderless, and the captain getting frustrated that he or she has not found the right port.

Vision is more than a business plan; it involves creating an image of your future. Your brain works off images. If you do not have an image of what you truly want to work toward in your recruiting business, your brain will default into a mode of simply fulfilling a need. "I am filling a need to take care of my bills." "I am filling a need to take care of my family." There is nothing wrong and no judgment with fulfilling these needs; these are valid concerns for people.

Imagine a bell curve. Eight-five to ninety percent of people are in the middle, and they are doing okay. They are paying their bills. They might not have the abundance of all of the things they want, but they "can't complain," or they believe they are limited by the economy, their niche, or their clients. Many in "the middle" are okay, but they *know* there is more possible for them. They just are not clear on what is out there.

To truly reach another level, you need to go beyond need by asking yourself the following questions:

1. "What has to be true for me to play a bigger game in my business?"

2. "What has to be true for me to work with only the types of clients who know, like, and respect me?" (When I say respect me, I mean that these clients work with your process and get back to you with timely feedback, and you fill most of the openings you take with them even if it is on contingency.)

If you are building a recruiting firm, you also want to ask these questions:

1. "What has to be true for you to play the role I want to be in?"

2. "Do I eventually want to get myself off of a desk?"

3. "Do I want to build a business that can run without me? If so, what would this allow me to do in both my personal and professional life?"

Many people get stuck when answering these questions because their response is, "I do not know how." You may not know how right now, but you also have to make a commitment and say that you will go through a process and figure it out over the next twelve, twenty-four, or thirty-six months. You must be truly committed to having this in your life and business! Once you answer these questions for yourself, it is time to build your clear, written vision for your business and life.

The vision should be precise about what it looks like when completed. Many people incorporate "shoulds" or other people's definitions of success into their visions. A vision is something that is in complete alignment with your desire. Remember, your brain works off of images. You can create your image of the future life and recruiting business aligned with your desires, or you can install what you think you "should" do and remain bored, frustrated, and joyless. The decision is entirely up to you.

When developing your vision, be intentional. Perhaps you want to get off a desk because you desire to build a firm where everyone else is harvesting new accounts and you are the leader, trainer, and developer. What is that broader vision for you? From there, you can get more specific.

Say you were going to build a custom home. During your first meeting with an architect, you describe what you want in your home. The master bedroom suite looks like this, and the bathrooms look like that. The family room will have this much space, and the kitchen will have this view. You talk about finding a piece of property on a lake, in the woods, in the city – whatever that is for you. The result is a vivid description of the lifestyle you want the architect to create in your new home. The architect then takes that vision you have for your home and creates a blueprint around it.

Describing your vision for the new home is the first step. Imagine just going to an architect and saying, "I want a three-bedroom, two-bathroom home. That is it." There is no way the architect can deliver plans that will meet your expectations with that information.

Recruiting firm owners share that they want to be the billing manager in a firm with three other recruiters working on their desk. They do not talk about their clients, revenue, or role. This conversation is the recruiting firm example of a three-bedroom, two-bathroom home.

If you were sitting down with a "recruiting firm architect," how would you describe that vision even though you do not know how to build it right now? That is the first step in creating your vision. Once you finish that, you can then take inventory of the gaps in knowledge and the systems and strategies you need to get there.

## WHAT ARE THE COMPONENTS OF A CLEAR, WRITTEN VISION?

Now that you have a concrete definition of your vision, you can now tackle creating a clear vision for your future. Your vision is the blueprint from which you will create your future based upon clear images that describe your blueprint's components in intricate detail. Where do you go from there? What are the components?

### *The Jigsaw Puzzle Metaphor of Vision*

When it comes to creating a vision for your future, the first step of this process is to ask yourself what your recruiting firm looks like. What are you building? From there, create images of you executing in that role.

A great way to start thinking about the components of vision is with a metaphor. On a rainy weekend some time ago, when my daughter was probably four or five years old, we pulled out a jigsaw puzzle and emptied all of the pieces on the table. Question: If you are going to complete a puzzle, right after you dump out all the pieces onto the table, what is the first thing you do?

When I ask people this question, they usually say that they turn all the pieces over so the color side is up and then separate all the edge pieces from the center. While those actions are all parts of the process, it is not the first thing you do. The first thing you do is look at the box top. Before you even begin sorting through the puzzle pieces, you want to know what the puzzle will look like when completed. Is it an ocean or mountain scene? Maybe it is a picture of a famous work of art. With that knowledge, you can say, "Okay, these pieces look like the sky, and these look like sand and an umbrella." You must start organizing the pieces so it all makes sense as you put the puzzle together.

Here is the critical thing: several studies have proven the correlation between how the brain processes activity versus imagination. One study by Aaron Berkowitz and David Ansari utilized functional magnetic resonance imagery (fMRI) to map how the brain functions when playing music versus imagining playing music. The fMRI scans revealed that the brain processed actual activity and improvised or imagined activity much in the same way. If you create vivid images about yourself in a role – earning a certain amount of money, taking certain types of vacations – and you imagine them seriously and intently, you will create the experience in your brain. I challenge you to do that as the first step. Create vivid images of your vision. Find your box top.

Here are some questions you should answer when envisioning your life and business three years from now:

- Three years from now, what is the role you *specifically* want to play in your business?

- If you are a solo recruiter, tell me about your *ideal* role with your clients three years from now?

- If your vision is to build a firm with recruiters who are

consistently producing, what is your role? Is it training, mentoring, and coaching?

• Are you still working a desk? If so, do you still want to be on a desk?

• If you stay on a desk, what is the role you want to have on the desk? If your genuine desire is to remain on your desk, look at the functions, roles, and titles you are searching on.

• Do you want to continue to do the marketing, or you want people feeding you leads?

• Do you want to continue recruiting candidates, or do you want to be managing the deal?

Once you have a clear vision of your role in your business, take the next step and look at your client relationships. With your business set up precisely as you wish, what do your clients look like three years from now? What current clients have you fired that no longer exist three years from now?

From there, clarify your revenue targets. What does your *ideal* revenue look like three years from now? You want exact numbers, not, "Oh, about a million," or, "About $400,000 as a solo operator." Make the revenue target specific. "I want to have a $1.5 million firm and 40 percent profits yielding these specific things, outcomes, and experiences in my life." Develop robust mental pictures and images like this. If these images do not bring positive emotions along with them, you are not specific enough or do not want them enough!

Specificity is critical when creating your vision for financial goals because it leads to the next question. Based on the vision you created for their business, what kind of lifestyle are you going to have? Will you have defined long weekends in your role? What types of vacations will you take? Specifically, where are you going to travel? Don't just say that you are going to take two nice vacations each year. Exactly where will these vacations occur? Are they at a lake or an ocean? If they are in the Caribbean, which island? Will you go to these islands on a cruise or a plane? If they are in Europe, which European countries will you visit? You can even go as far as planning out these trips. Go online and research resorts and excursions to create vivid images of the vacations you will be taking.

Finally, three years from now, think about what has to be true for you to have all those things you just wrote and work 25 precent less. All of this is possible. We have done this same exercise with our clients.

What has to be true for you to create incremental growth over the next three years while simultaneously decreasing the amount of physical time? When building a vision, most people subconsciously believe that doubling their revenue equals doubling their effort. When done the right way, doubling your revenue can often be done at 25 percent less effort – even if you get conservative, 10 percent less – because it ultimately requires less of your time.

It is effortless to get caught up in the how when creating a vision, which is why many people do not create bold visions for themselves and their businesses. They get caught up in how to make their vision a reality before they even begin the process of gaining *vivid clarity* of their true desires. Start with what you want. We will show you how; the how will show up.

## CREATING A TIMEFRAME FOR YOUR VISION

The questions I share reference three years from now. Three years is sufficient. However, I always challenge people to look as far out as five years. Some people have trouble grasping that, so I back into three years. Even at three years, I have clients who feel unsure about the process, especially those who have never gone through the vision-creation process.

If you cannot imagine things three years out, start by looking out one year. What I like about three years is that it is beyond your reach of executing right now. If you have what Jim Collins refers to as a BHAG (Big, Hairy, Audacious Goal), looking at it from the perspective of three years out, you give yourself ample time to get started right now. The journey of a thousand miles starts with a single step. If you can see your goal's realization is three years from now, you are giving yourself the cushion of time to implement it.

Once you set your goal, you can then reverse engineer the steps to achievement. "If I achieve this in three years, what must be true twelve months from now?" From there, you can plan the projects necessary to make incremental progress toward your goal. Essentially, you will define what projects you need to execute over the next quarter and the next month and then drill that down to actions needed for each week.

## HOW YOUR VISION ALIGNS WITH CERTAIN REVENUE

You may feel tempted quit on yourself if you establish a revenue goal in the absence of a vision. By quitting, I mean that when you are faced with challenges while implementing new strategies or techniques, you might consider taking a step back into old habits. For example, you may start doing things to get money upfront and face rejection. Without a clear vision of why converting your recruiting practice from mostly contingent to mostly engaged or retained is good, you may resort to accepting what work you can get. Nothing works 100 percent of the time, but when you clarify why you are making these changes, you will want to fight for the vision you created.

The beauty of the recruiting industry is that financial vision has an exact, specific, and precise amount of activity that you – or you and your team – need to generate for revenue fulfillment.

## GETTING CLEAR ON CLARITY OF VISION

Creating a clear, written vision for your future is an incredibly creative process. As with all creative processes, you might not complete it in one sitting. We have shared several questions you can ask yourself to help guide you through the process. Grab a blank legal pad, and coffee, tea, or a relaxing beverage of your choice. Put on some music in the background. Give yourself an hour or three one-hour blocks over the next couple weeks, and start filling in the blanks around all those questions I asked you before. Get crystal clear on what you want for yourself without any "shoulds."

When answering the questions, the key is to be specific in your answers and write them as if you already achieved your goals. Write as if the vision is already complete – "I already have these things." You will then see a natural gap with where you are currently and natural starting points. For example, if one of your goals is to take two vacations this year, write out in incredible detail what those vacations will be. It might be: the first vacation will be a seven-day, six-night vacation at the Sheraton on Maui in March; a stay in an oceanfront room; and a hiking excursion in the rainforest.

The second vacation will be a five-day, four-night trip to Iceland in October, where you stay at the Hotel Rangá to watch the Northern Lights from the hot tub on the balcony of your room. The key is to create as many images as you can around your goals.

Once you fill in the blanks and define the things as if you already have them, reverse engineer how you will achieve your goals. Define the first three steps you can take to move closer toward your vision, whether it is twelve or thirty-six months from now.

As you go through each chapter in this book, we will show you that each part of your business directly correlates with your vision. Creating a clear, written vision is the foundation to achieving Certain Revenue, becoming a preferred partner with all your clients, and going from founder dependent to a team-run business. Those outcomes are all possible with Clarity of Vision.

# CLARITY OF VISION CASE STUDY

## BOB SEMINERIO – SCI INTERNATIONAL

Bob is the managing partner of the Pharma and Healthcare Technology Practice at SCI International, located in northern New Jersey. He and his team recruit director to C-level roles. Bob has been a The RecruiterU client since 2011 and used the power of Clarity of Vision to grow his desk and scale his team.

## WHAT DOES CLARITY OF VISION MEAN TO YOU?

The best way for me to describe Clarity of Vision is just how I look at it from a day-to-day basis, meaning looking at the overall, bigger picture. I start by thinking, "Okay, what do I want from this experience?"

Whether it is professionally, personally, or both, I go through the same process. That process begins with sitting down and really going through the entire exercise of writing out a five-year plan or a seven-year plan of what I am setting out to achieve in almost ridiculous detail. If it is a new car you want, how do the rims look? What color is it? Describe the interior in detail as much detail as possible. That is kind of a bigger picture – being very clear about what you want.

When I first did this, I was younger, probably late twenties. I was talking to Mike about the future house I wanted to buy. He challenged me to envision this house not just in the macro details but the micro details as well. We discussed the obvious details of how many bedrooms and bathrooms. Then, he asked me to go deeper. What does the deck look like? How many garages does it have? What is the interior layout? Again, the more detail that I can get into, I find the better it is and the clearer it will be.

For me, getting down to, like, a day-to-day and how I know it is my true vision is when I am just in the middle of my day... Maybe I have had a frustrating call or something like that, or even just a routine call – whatever. When I am in the middle of my day, when I am looking, when I go back in memory, and I think of what do I want, what is that clear vision? It must align exactly with what I have written down.

I have found that if I get a little bit off track from my vision, I do not achieve my goals quickly.

But when what I am doing is aligned with my vision,

things happen and happen quickly. I have done this probably three or four times now throughout my career. I have set seven-year plans and five-year plans. I remember the first two seven-year visions that I put out there. I think they were achieved within three or four years.

It is really the clarity of what it is that you truly want. You have got to be able to think of it on a second's notice – just on a regular, random, every old day. That is the best way I can explain it from a macro and a day-to-day vision.

## HOW DID CLARITY OF VISION CHANGE YOUR BUSINESS?

Whenever I am looking to achieve something, I have had different steps and progress as far as scaling the business. For a while, it was just myself, and then we added team members from there. Each step along the way, I have noticed if I have plateaued for maybe a year or a couple of years – which I have a couple of times – I plateau. That plateau usually occurs the year or two after I have achieved the most recent vision. At that point, I have not then come back to specifically resetting what it is that I want.

Sometimes, it takes me a little while to really understand what it is that I want. The next Clarity of Vision might not be clear to you right away. Sometimes, it might have to marinate for a little while, or you achieve something, and then, "Okay, what is next?" Some people may come upon their vision more quickly than I have, but I have noticed when I have Clarity of Vision, I will move right and hit it. And then after that, if I do not have one right away, I kind of plateau there.

When I have a clear vision, I do not necessarily know how I will get there. (This is important! The *how* does *not* show up until you commit to your vision!) I just start moving in that direction toward the vision, and I usually end up hitting it in a more efficient time manner than I even put out there for myself. Clarity of Vision has been important because I notice when I do not have it, I kind of plateau; when I do, I am going laser-focused, right at it there.

If you are not sure what to do, really, getting clarity around that vision is exactly what will propel you toward it.

You do not need to know how you will achieve your vision necessarily, but you need to have a vision in place. That vision has got to be something, I think, that you are really feeling on a daily basis. If it is just, "I would like to fly around the world," okay, great. I do not know what that means, and you are probably not going to do it because you have not necessarily put it into that ridiculous detail. But if you have an idea of what that is, just the fact that you have the clarity, I think, is going to propel you in that direction. Without it, you are probably just going to coast or meander along.

## ANY LAST THOUGHTS ABOUT CLARITY OF VISION THAT YOU WOULD LIKE TO SHARE?

I would just say that your vision has really got to be something that is truly meaningful to you. Your vision is not something that can be what you think someone else wants for you or something you should do, be doing, or have done. I think your vision has really got to be something that means something to you.

If your vision does not truly resonate with you, as far as what you really want and where you want to take your business or personal relationships, whatever, I do not really think it will work. Clarity of Vision does not have to be just a business thing, but unless it is clear and really means something to you, it will not work.

You have got to have those two things. If you do – and I notice when I have clarity aligned with my desire, things just fall into place – you are, like, speeding through it. And when you are not, you are just coasting along there. You couple the clarity with the fact that it has really got to mean something to you.

5

# RECRUITER GPS

The next step in creating a *real* recruiting business is what I call Recruiter GPS. Think about the GPS on your phone. If you want to go from New York City to Los Angeles, the only thing you need to know is where you currently are and where you would like to be. Just like you would use Google Maps in your car, you are going to a destination that you might not have gone to before or have not gone too often. The navigation will tell you to turn right here, turn left here, or go ten miles on the same route. Eventually, you end up at your destination because you were guided there by a navigation device.

Recruiter GPS is a coined The RecruiterU term, commonly referred to as metrics or key performance indicators (KPIs). It is the key numbers we measure that predict your income. Unfortunately, most recruiters either do not know this intellectually or do not know this at all. It is not your fault! Once you jump into your recruiting vehicle (your business), Recruiter GPS will guide you through which turns you have to take and what directions you have to go to take that 3,000-mile journey toward your next destination.

## THE IMPORTANCE OF METRICS AND CERTAIN REVENUE

Most recruiters and recruiting firm owners have been trained to track placements. The obvious reason to track placements is because that is where revenue is generated. The only problem with defining your success week to week and month to month based on the number of placements you make is that you're creating a definition of success on the one thing that you have absolutely no control over! You have no control over whether a client makes an offer or whether the candidate accepts that offer.

Granted, you have a strong influence on your clients through conversations. There are things you can say to your clients who influence the structure and timing of the offer. You can also do things with candidates to influence their ability to accept an offer based on the numbers, situation, timing, et cetera.

However, you only have influence; you do not have any control. Even though you do not have control over the placement, when the deal blows up, you – at some level – define yourself as a failure. The negative self-talk that occurs may sound like, "I cannot do this business." This feeling is especially true when you are new to the business and believe your inability to put the deal together was your fault. While there may have been things that contributed to an unfavorable outcome, again – I cannot stress this enough – the placement is beyond your control.

What is in your control then? In your control are all the things that lead up to a placement. These things include the number of candidates and prospects you talk to, the number of interviews you arrange, and the number of job orders you take. You might say that you cannot control if a company has an opening. Correct, that is out of your control too. However, you can control your ability to implement the amount of marketing activity that leads to a job order. While KPIs or metrics are essential for any business, many recruiters neglect using metrics in their practice.

The reason solo recruiters and recruiting firm owners neglect to use Recruiter GPS is ignorance. Most people have an awareness of metrics. Even though I was taught the meaning and power of tracking my activity, I was never taught how metrics provide complete sanity, predictability, and control over my revenue.

Imagine a billion-dollar publicly traded corporation has an earnings call, and the CEO says: "Our goal was $250 million last quarter. We did not hit our numbers because Bob in San Diego quit, and we lost Mary in Chicago too!" You will never hear of individual sales performance as a reason for not meeting the target. In an average economy, any large corporation can predict their income within a penny or two, most often per share. How do they do that? They use the same concepts in this chapter. These concepts pertain to all recruiting practice structures, whether it is a $250,000 desk or a $10 million firm.

Most recruiting firm owners do not track and hold their recruiters accountable to metrics because they believe it is a form of micromanagement. They said, "My people are adults. I should not need to do that." Every other company in the country runs off KPIs or metrics. Why should your recruiting practice be any different?

Instead of using metrics as a punishment, I will show you how to use them as a path to liberation for your recruiters. The beauty of metrics is if you execute your targets week to week and month to month, you cannot help but hit your annual income goals. Ignorance of this fact is the number one reason solo recruiters and recruiting firm owners do not track metrics or KPIs. This ignorance holds them back from gaining complete sanity and predictability on a recruiting desk and in a recruiting firm.

## YOUR PERSONAL RECRUITER GPS

The reason metrics are so easy to install in your recruiting practice is because there are only four critical data points to measure. Those data points are marketing presentations (MP), recruit presentations (RP), job orders (JO), and first-time interviews (FTI).

An MP is actual interaction with somebody in a position to hire. This conversation can be on the phone, via video, or in person. An MP is not an email or text exchange, and voice-mail does not count. What does count is calling someone, presenting your services, and having a conversation, regardless of the length of the conversation or outcome. The conversation can be as quick as, "We never use recruiters," and they hang up. As long as you get the other person on the phone, that counts as one presentation.

An RP is an actual conversation with a candidate about moving forward in their career. Still, it is not a follow-up conversation with a candidate that you already presented an opportunity to. The same as MPs, this conversation can be on the phone, via video, or in person, and emails, text exchanges, and voicemails do not count. The conversation can be as quick as, "I hate recruiters. Goodbye," and they hang up. As long as you get the other person on the phone, that counts as one presentation.

A note on MPs and RPs: If you have an MP or RP with someone and it is five minutes into it, and they say, "You know what, I want to continue this conversation, but I am out of time. Can we finish this call tomorrow?" and you have another call tomorrow, it only counts as one. The second call with that person is a continuation of the first, not a new conversation.

Our definition of a JO is a search assignment you will work on. We do not include any JOs you take at poor fees or terms that you will not do anything with. An FTI is the first meeting between the client and candidate. This interview can be on the phone, via video, or in person.

## GOAL SETTING WITH METRICS MADE EASY

It is straightforward to reverse engineer your activity goals. To begin, you will need the revenue number you wish to bill and your average fee. I will use some standard numbers in this example. Remember that this formula works for any revenue target.

Reverse engineer the activity targets for a $250,000 desk with an average fee of $21,000. Most people have a higher or lower average fee, but $21,000 is average across multiple niches and levels of search from our experience. Mathematically, this will result in total revenue of $252,000. Using simple math, a goal of $250,000 with an average fee of $21,000 means you need to make twelve placements in a year, or one placement per month.

Conservatively, we can assume that for every eight FTIs you arrange – regardless of if they are on the phone, over video chat, or in person – will result in o placement. I prefer to use an 8:1 FTI-to-placement ratio with clients who have not tracked metrics in the past. Carrying on with assumptions based on years of working with clients, a conservative ratio for RP to FTI is 12:1, which means you need to have twelve candidate conversations for one person to go out on an interview.

Moving onto the JO to placement ratio, if you are contingency, it is not uncommon for every four JOs you take to fill one. A retained desk JO-to-placement ratio is 4:3 or 5:4. For this example, we are going to work with the contingency ratio of 4:1.

Our experience is in this market is that it takes about thirteen MPs to get one JO. If you are a more seasoned recruiter, that ratio might be lower. Again, for the sake of this example, we are using very conservative numbers.

Based on all of the above assumptions and factoring activity over forty-eight weeks, this is what the activity on a $250,000 desk with an average fee of $21,000 looks like:

- Revenue goal = $250,000

- Average fee = $21,000

- Assuming:

    - FTI:PL = 8:1
    - RP:FTI = 15:1
    - JO:PL = 5:1
    - MP:JO = 13:1

- 12 Placements needed to achieve revenue goal ($250,000 ÷ $21,000 average fee)

- 96 FTIs needed per year (12 placements 8 interviews)

    - 2 FTIs are needed per week (96 ÷ 48 weeks)

- 1,440 RPs are needed per year (96 FTIs 15 RP to yield 12 placements)

    - 28 RPs are needed per week

- 60 JOs are needed per year (12 placements 5 JOs)
- 780 MPs needed per year (60 JOs 13 MPs)
- 16.25 marketing presentations MPs per week

The formula above is the exact mathematical equation used to reverse engineer the activity needed to generate $250,000 in revenue per year. You would need to talk to twenty-eight recruits and fifteen to sixteen prospects per week. That's a total of forty-four to forty-five conversations each week with an average of nine conversations a day between RP and MP combined.

The challenge is most people do not have even two or three conversations, MP, RP, or a combination of the two, each day. They always are focused on their deals in progress versus executing these targets. Tracking your daily metrics is just as easy as defining your goals using our simple math formula.

There are no sophisticated systems needed to keep track of your activity. I built a $3 million business using three-by-three Post-It notes for my recruiters to track their numbers. You can use whatever tracking method works best for you, whether that is a Post-It note or a complex tracking system.

If you choose to use a Post-It note, write M, T, W, T, F at the top, and MP, RP, JO down the left-hand side. From there, make a hash mark each time you complete the activity. I like a small Post-It pad or any small pad of paper because they do not take up a lot of space in your desk. I also find the act of making that hash mark is very motivating. It feels very similar to the dopamine response of crossing off a task on a to-do list.

Some software, such as your CRM or ATS (applicant tracking system), have embedded metrics tracking capabilities. My experience with these is that the process is not streamlined and requires you to go back through two or more screens to close your activity. The beauty of low-tech solutions is both speed and accuracy.

One technology I do encourage is software that is dedicated only to metrics tracking. We developed a custom portal for our clients to enter their numbers. The process of entering your numbers into the portal takes less than five minutes each week, not each day. There are also a variety of other similar services that will track your metrics.

The bottom line is your CRM can track your metrics, but all you need is a Post-It pad. At the end of the week, add up your totals for each of the metrics, and measure your goal versus actual. If you utilize software for tracking, enter in your actual numbers in less than five minutes. Go into your weekly numbers, and it is that simple.

## GETTING STARTED WITH RECRUITER GPS

Installing Recruiter GPS in your practice requires nothing more than some primary data, a calculator, the formula we outlined, and a Post-It note or even a scrap piece of paper.

To get started, go back to the formula and change the numbers appropriately. Your goal may be lower at or higher than our example. You also need to know your average fee, which is easy to determine. Look at the last six invoices you generated, total them up and divide them by six. You may not know your ratios, such as FTI to placement. In that case, use the assumptions we provided as a baseline benchmark.

You will have reliable data within four weeks of consistent metrics tracking regarding how many candidates it takes to get an interview and how many prospects to talk to get a JO. If you track that, you will have enough data in a month to have highly forecastable revenue. Just take out a piece of paper, create goals using our worst-case scenario ratios as a baseline, and start making hash marks. Do all of this, and you will be on track in no time.

I challenge you to stop tracking placements as your sole metric of success and start tracking the activity that leads to the placement. Do not allow ignorance or a belief that tracking metrics is micromanagement to hold you back. These beliefs are the reasons people do not track metrics even after we reveal their real power. It is like someone trying to lose weight but not getting on a scale. You do not want to see what the number is. But remaining blissfully unaware does not mean your production will be any better. It just allows you to deny yourself the truth of what you are accomplishing. Instead, determine your activity goals and begin to define your success or failure each week as, "Did I execute to those targets? "This way, you *know* if you are on target to hit your annual numbers EACH WEEK!

I do not expect you to be perfect, but seeing where you are on a daily basis allows you to course correct in days, not months. This will shorten your slumps, increase your focus, and help you identify when the day is *done!*

# RECRUITER GPS DESK-LEVEL CASE STUDY

## ARDITH RADEMACHER – ARDITH RADEMACHER AND ASSOCIATES

Ardith is the owner of Ardith Rademacher and Associates, a boutique recruiting firm based in San Antonio, Texas, servicing the construction industry. Ardith has been a client of The RecruiterU since 2013.

In this case study, Ardith shares how metrics and Recruiter GPS allowed her to grow her individual billings and add recruiters to her firm.

## WHAT DO METRICS MEAN TO YOU?

Let's start with what I used to think it meant to me. When I first heard "metrics," it meant tracking stuff. It did not have meaning because I did not understand why Recruiter GPS was relevant, and I did not understand why additional data would just be important.

Metrics are now a North Star to me because it is not about them being immediately applicable. My metrics all specifically align to exactly and precisely what I want to do in a year, and they are then reverse engineered to what that looks like on my desk every single day and what my monthly plans look like because they are rolling up into my quarterly plans, which are rolling into my annual plan. I never knew a metric could do that. I thought it was just a math thing you chased.

I did not realize that metrics were like a living, breathing map to tell you, "Look at where you have been, and understand how you got there and how the numbers literally make the path forward using those markers that you have left in the past." Then, you predict and plan for growth, whether as a solo recruiter or not, in getting from this "amount" of billings to this amount of billings using those numbers, and then that is how you also grow a team.

I was a very late starter to metrics. It was not – again, it did not mean anything to me. Probably one of the first things I ever took away with working with Mike and The RecruiterU was how Recruiter GPS actually aligned with me, what it meant to me, and how I got them.

As soon as I hit that, I mean, it flipped a switch. I will tell you, it was so clear that in the first year that I was introduced to metrics, it tripled my billings. It was actually 311 percent of what I had been doing because I did not even know what to look at before. And it was not more work. It was actually less work that year than all the other years I had worked before.

## HOW DID RECRUITER GPS HELP YOU GROW YOUR BUSINESS?

In growing and scaling the business, what Recruiter GPS allowed me to do was get really clear on a common language with new employees that we could all, again, use as a North Star that we would all understand and work toward.

What that allowed me to do with somebody brand new was tell them basically how they could meet their goals as they aligned with the organization's goals and my goals and then help them understand how the metrics would do that. And then, I held them accountable to the metrics. Because as a new employee and somebody maybe coming into this industry, they did not understand them in the same way I did not understand them, and they did not have the history I did on my desk. So, the metrics for growing a team were really fantastic in improving clarity around what a person's job was going to be and what success looked like in that job and then holding themselves accountable to it.

I liken knowing metrics and accountability metrics to using a FitBit or an Apple Watch to track your steps. If a person sets a goal for themselves and they know that hitting that goal is a certain number of steps, then they know, yes or no, if they hit it or they did not hit it. If it is 4:00 p.m. and they are at 2,000 steps, they are either walking until midnight, or they are just like, "I did not get it." If you are standing next to them – let's say that you will know when they hit their 10,000th step because they are doing a little jig. That is really what metrics and Recruiter GPS are.

Metrics allow me to understand what I need from my company to hit the company's goals. Each individual on my team has a personal goal that is their own. It is a goal that means something to them in their life and their personal goals. The metrics allow them to see how they are meeting their goals and to see how they are aligned with the organization. And honestly, it is a way of rewarding them without actually having to say, "Way to go!" every single day because they know that they have done it.

Implementing Recruiter GPS in your firm is also a really great way of managing hard discussions because it is data. At some point, they chose not to do the metrics, and when they made that choice, they decided about their own goals and the goals they had with this team. This has made that piece of it a lot easier too.

## DO YOU FINDING THAT TRACKING YOUR METRICS IS CHALLENGING?

Oh no. It's actually something I look forward to now. I have kept my metrics on, literally, a Post-It note next to my desk – the hash marks – and then once a week, I load it into a portal. Every week, I am looking at that and adjusting the numbers. That number is a dynamic system.

In other words, based on our goals, what has changed? Maybe our fees have gotten higher, so we might need fewer first-time interviews. Or maybe if we hold to our first-time interviews, we can adjust our revenue goals. Do we see something in the market that we need more marketing calls to get opportunities? Are we seeing something change in the market where we need a lot more recruiting calls to get the candidates to fill a job? Week by week, it allows us to really adjust our rudder and also gives us a great bellwether on what the market is doing. Maybe it is just spring break in that particular area we are working at, or if we start seeing something that runs more than a couple of weeks, then maybe we are seeing something shift in an industry.

Recruiter GPS has actually allowed us to scale the business. Since we started growing the team, we have continued to scale the overall goals in ways that I would never have expected. I mean, I surprise myself all the time with that. Like, wow, it works. I mean, you put this number down, you hold yourself accountable to daily and weekly *activity* numbers, and you get the *billing* number every single time.

# RECRUITER GPS FIRM-LEVEL CASE STUDY

## TIFFANY HOFFINE – AQUANTUS

Tiffany Hoffine is the managing partner of AquantUs, located in midtown Atlanta. AquantUs specializes in recruiting accounting and finance professionals at all levels, both direct hire and interim consulting. Tiffany has been in recruiting since 2003 and started AquantUs in 2009.

## WHAT DO METRICS MEAN TO YOU?

Metrics is one of my favorite topics. Both my husband, who is also my business partner, and I are accountants by training. We are both CPAs who grew up in Deloitte, one of the Big Four accounting firms, so metrics really speak to us in our workflow.

We embraced Recruiter GPS and metrics from the start and have been on a journey with metrics. Like everything else, we have gotten a lot smarter. The metrics evolved for us and continue to evolve. But at the end of the day, what metrics mean to us is it really allows us to have visibility at the desk level at our firm. Still, it also allows us to, at times, disappear and have this measuring stick where we know what is happening without having to be physically here to inspect everything.

The very short answer to that is metrics to us as firm owners mean freedom.

## CAN YOU SHARE A BIT OF WHAT THAT FREEDOM IS FOR YOU? WHAT DO YOU DO WITH THAT FREEDOM?

When we first started AquantUs, we definitely felt like we needed to be physically there with the team every day. Every placement was a surprise, and every "not" placement was a surprise. Once we dialed into metrics – the canary in the coal mine, if you will, for us, is first-time interviews. We have it down to a science where, for us, in our business and our market, we know with near certainty that we will make a placement on the direct hire side for every eight first-time interviews we arrange.

The number of first-time interviews, of course, can vary with other firms based upon what their specialty and market is, but for us, we can tell a recruiter or business development person with close to 100 percent certainty that if you can schedule eight first-time interviews, you will make a placement.

We use metrics in one of two ways. One is backward-looking when we meet with each of our recruiters and business development folks weekly to say, "Okay, what did you do last week? What do you need to do more of this week?"

When metrics are used properly, they also become very predictive. It is like, okay, based on the number of interviews you have arranged, we know you have X placements coming up. Based on your interview activity, you will be making three placements over the next three to five weeks.

Recruiter GPS provides us, as business owners, visibility – not only into the day-to-day of what the team is doing, but it allows us to forecast revenues very, very accurately. The team is also really embracing metrics because it allows them to see, "Okay, here is what I have in my pipeline. Here is how many placements I have ongoing. Uh-oh, the pipeline is drying up; I definitely need to get more first interviews scheduled." Then, we back into, "What do you, as a recruiter or a business development manager, need to do every single day to meet your goals?"

## HOW HAS RECRUITER GPS CHANGED YOUR BUSINESS OVERALL, ESPECIALLY IN YOUR FIRM STRUCTURE, HIRING, RETENTION, AND OTHER ASPECTS OF YOUR BUSINESS?

Right now, when you and I are talking, we are in a fully remote situation because of COVID-19. Before COVID-19, we were all in the office 100 percent. Before metrics, I definitely felt like I needed to be there every day, the team needs to be there every day, and there was definitely this feeling like they better be here at a certain time and better be there until a certain time.

Metrics provided my recruiters and me the freedom that when we pulled the plug in March 2020 and sent everyone home to work fully remotely – which we had never done – metrics were really a saving grace for us and our recruiters. I did not have eyes on them every day, but I still got my daily reports as to what they were doing. I still felt connected to them and the work. It allowed me to step back and say, "Okay, I don't need to micromanage what this person is doing every hour, every minute, when they're coming, when they're leaving, as long as they meet these KPIs or metrics."

When we sent everyone home to work remotely, had we not had metrics, I think that would have been a much more difficult situation from a management perspective and an individual recruiter perspective. I do not know that they would have known how they were doing if we had not already had strong metrics in place.

The COVID-19 office shutdown has undoubtedly opened up our eyes that we do not need to be in the office every day. The team does not need to be here every day. I think that realization is providing a lot more freedom for us as owners and managers and the team as far as where and when they can work. The team, like they said – they do not see metrics as a micromanagement tool. They see it as their own predictive tool.

We have some automated reports that get emailed to them, and if those are held up for any reason, we have the team calling us, saying, "Where are my metrics?" because they really love having that. Recruiter GPS is the certainty of revenue. For them, they know if they do those activities, this work will follow. Sometimes, with first interviews, like everyone else, you have a little bit of a dry spell, and it keeps people motivated because they are like, "I am booking the interviews. I may be on a little bit of a delay, but I know this will eventually settle right back at eight first interviews to a placement." Maybe in the short term, that spikes up to ten or twelve or even sixteen, then they make three placements in a week, and it comes right back down to the firm average.

## ANY LAST THOUGHTS YOU WOULD LIKE TO SHARE?

I know that I have talked to other firm owners who have been hesitant to implement metrics because they feel like it would be perceived as micromanaging. My experience is it is all probably in the rollout. But if we, as firm owners, embrace Recruiter GPS as a way to more freedom for ourselves and more freedom for our team, the team will do the same.

For any firm owners who are perhaps hesitant to implement metrics because of that fear of how it is going to be perceived by the team, I think it can absolutely be done in a way where it is embraced by the team, individual recruiters, and business development folks or full-desk folks if that is the way you manage your firm. They see it as a positive and a motivator. For us, as firm owners, when we really got into metrics, it was transformative to our own job satisfaction and the team. If any firm owners are hesitant, think about it that way. It is freedom, not micromanaging.

6

# FOCUSED PLANNING

"The devil fools with the best-laid plans."

— NEIL YOUNG

## THE MOST COMMON REASONS WHY PLANS FAIL

The reason that most plans fail is that they are *boring*. Plans are boring for two specific reasons: (1) people do not understand the level of importance of them, and (2) in recruiting, they are done horribly. These are observations from the personal lens of being a recovering horrible planner.

Planning is such a challenge for recruiters because the outcome that you want (the placement) is so distant from the activity needed to make that placement. The very activity you plan to do today or this week –marketing, recruiting, and first-time interviews – is not money in your bank account for ninety days.

There is such a lag between the actual activity you plan and the actual outcome of making a placement and getting the check, which is unique to the recruiting profession. This lag provides ample opportunities for daily procrastination without any immediate negative consequences.

For the most part, recruiters do not know how to plan. I think people that are good at recruiting, but most find that actually mapping out a plan is boring. Recruiters are great at talking to people, finding the right candidate, arranging the interview, and closing the deal. However, neglecting to create a clear vision, calculate the metrics to achieve your revenue goals, and plan will result in unpredictable income.

Planning is bringing your Clarity of Vision and Recruiter GPS together to create the specific outcome you desire. Planning is reverse engineering the numbers. From there, you will know exactly, specifically, and precisely what your activity for the week needs to be.

## HOW TO DEVELOP A HABIT OF PLANNING

The first step in developing a habit of planning is by creating a clear written vision. Before you begin the planning process, review your vision. What is it that you want for yourself that you have an emotional connection to, both personally and professionally, in your life? How is what you are doing as a recruiter tying into that vision? Many people say they want financial freedom, but they have not yet defined what financial freedom means to them. Make sure you have absolute clarity in each area of desire you wrote about in your vision.

Know what those components are from the vision, and then bring each element down to what needs to happen a year, three months, next month, and next week to achieve this goal from my vision in three- or five-years' time. In the absence of a vision, a plan is somewhat random.

## THE FIVE COMPONENTS OF FOCUSED PLANNING

There are five components to all successful plans, with each plan building upon the other.

### *Annual Plan*

An annual plan includes one-year goals. A mentor of mine, Dan Sullivan, asked this question: "What has to be true for you, both personally and professionally, twelve months from now for you to be thrilled with your progress?"

The answer to that question guides you through developing an annual plan. I answer that question in the *past* tense (as if it has already been achieved) as it pertains to your role, your revenue, the types of clients you worked with, and the type of personal life you had. From there, use the simple formula from in Chapter 2 to define your Recruiter GPS on an annual basis.

For example, for you as an individual producer, your revenue goal may be to bill $300,000 with an average fee of $25,000 using the Recruiter GPS formula that requires one placement a month. If you assume an 8:1 interview-to-placement ratio, that means arranging eight interviews each month, or ninety-six total interviews in a year.

Once you define what success looks like in twelve-months' time and the activity needed to realize this success, you can move on to the next component of your annual plan, where you look at your current situation and your goal to identify any gaps. The question to ask yourself is, "Based on where I want to be twelve months from now, where are am I at right now?"

Another line Dan Sullivan has is, "All progress starts with telling the truth." The truth is all about data, not drama. Drama would be saying that you would have been better off "if those two deals did not blow up" or "if that company did not freeze those positions." The truth is the data, which usually links to a gap or several gaps existing in your business.

Take a hard look at your business. What gaps exist between where you are at now and where you want to be? Look at all twelve areas of the Recruiting Firm Optimizer Model. For each area, define the gap. Your gap analysis will reveal two or three, if not more, projects that you can work on straight away that will have an *immediate* impact. Once you define these larger projects' outcomes, you know have the beginnings of your quarterly plan.

### *Quarterly Plan*

Once you have defined the projects that address your gaps, those projects become the seeds of your quarterly/ninety-day projects. One gap you may have identified is that you are not tracking metrics. The way to successfully define a project, such as metrics tracking, is to define the specific outcome. A specific outcome is not, "I am going to track metrics this quarter." A specific outcome from that project is, "At the end of ninety days, we will have tracked all the KPIs and know our marketing-presentation-to-job-order ratio and recruit-presentation-to-first-time-interview ratio and will be able to forecast revenue ninety days out."

Once you have your specific outcome defined, determine measurable tasks or milestones toward completing the project. Still working with the metrics example, here is an example of the milestones for the project:

1. Track all KPIs daily.

2. Set up metrics tracking, software, or a portal.

3. Establish a policy for entering the numbers weekly. (You need a policy or protocol, especially for your team, that outlines how to track, the deadline to input their numbers, and the process for inputting.)

4. Review team numbers weekly and coach on gaps.

The example we have been working with of implementing metrics is a small quarterly project. However, it fulfills all of the requirements of a successful quarterly plan.

1. You have a specific outcome: "We will be able to forecast revenue by implementing metrics. We will complete the implementation within ninety days."

2. From the specific outcome, you created specific, measurable tasks or milestones.

Once you have created your quarterly plan and defined the projects with specific outcomes, measurable tasks, and milestones, the next logical step is to create a monthly plan.

*Monthly Plan*

The next step is to break the quarterly plan into a monthly plan and actions. The question to ask when developing a monthly plan is, "What do I want to accomplish for the month, both personally and professionally?" When asking yourself this question, start with a personal plan. Include how you will spend your free time and what your plan is for time with your family and any health-related activities you will engage in into the personal portion of your monthly plan.

On the professional side, determine how many first-time interviews are needed individually or as a firm for the month. Also, look at your quarterly plan and determine which quarterly projects you will start, continue to make incremental progress toward, or finish over the next month. From there, you can outline specifically what part of that project will be complete by the end of the month.

Once you create a monthly plan, distill that plan down to a weekly plan.

### *Weekly and Daily Plans*

The final two components of a successful plan are the weekly and daily plans. Let us revisit the example of an individual that wants $300,000 a year, which requires needs two first-time interviews each week. The primary question – perhaps the only question – is, "Where are my two first-time interviews coming from this week?"

If you do not have any searches to work on, your weekly plan will focus on marketing. On the flip side, if you have several open searches, your weekly plan will focus more on recruiting. The overall question you will be asking yourself each day is, "Where are my first-time interviews coming from this week?" The focus on first-time interviews may mean prioritizing the quality of the searches you are working on to increase your capacity to set up those two first-time interviews.

Based on how many searches or job orders you are working on, you can determine if you will lean more heavily on recruiting than marketing. From there, you can plan your activity according to the specific number of conversations needed in each category. That determination of the number of conversation types needed (marketing versus recruiting) will drive what you do each day.

Adding up all five of these components – annual plan, quarterly plan, monthly plan, weekly plan, and daily plan – equals your twelve-month outcome and is 33 percent of your three-year vision.

Once you create your plan, know that life happens. You might be wildly successful and have numerous job orders that you need to fill. You might also have a personal issue that comes up. How does one course correct when life happens?

When you make a bold commitment to yourself, something in your life is going to poke at you for its attention. I heard this from other mentors, and I did not believe it was true, but you can be making a bold commitment to go to another level, and something happens. Maybe your furnace blows up, and that is going to cost $5,000 or $10,000 to install. Regardless of the life event, you will be tempted to take your eye off the vision and plan you set for yourself.

When life happens – as it will – the question is, "How do I take care of this thing in my personal situation and maintain my commitment to what I want for myself?" Adapting to changing priorities or whatever life throws at you shows you over time that you can follow through. No one is going to be 100 percent every day. The goal is progress, not perfection.

I always advocate that if you have a bad day, do not go into the next day thinking that you will make up for the bad day. If you did not meet your activity targets on Monday, do not attempt to double your activity on Tuesday. Trying to make up for a bad day the following day is a recipe for failure. Instead, have a 100-percent day on Tuesday to prove to yourself that you can have a 100-percent day on Tuesdays. Build on that momentum, and then have a 100-percent day on Wednesday.

When you get off track and have a bad day – and you will – simply get back on track the next day.

Finally, when planning, especially when it comes down to making revenue targets, many people want to set realistic goals. The word "realistic" in my personal dictionary is "pessimistic." Let us talk about the reality, especially for people new to the business. If you are a brand-new recruiter and have never billed a dime, you have little to no idea what you are doing at first. When creating your vision and goals, you may decide that you want to bill one million dollars in your first year. However, you do not have Recruiter GPS to guide you yet. A million dollars is a realistic goal but most likely an unrealistic timeframe.

I do not ever think there is any such thing as an unrealistic goal. I *do* believe that there are unrealistic timeframes. Sometimes, in integrity, you will not know what a realistic timeframe is until you begin to execute it. There is no dishonor in that; it is a learning experience. If, in your heart, you said, "I did my very best, and I came up with X minus Y of production," perhaps that is the "realistic level." But that still feels like a copout to me, even in uncertain economic climates.

We see new people in the business or people struggling or in a real slump talk to fifteen people a day. These are conversations, not email, LinkedIn, or text exchanges – fifteen conversations a day. Now, most people say, "That is unrealistic." When you plan the right way for it, using the components detailed in this chapter, and maybe some outsourced research support, you make an unrealistic plan realistic.

Lastly, instead of using the word "realistic," ask yourself, "What has to be true for me to have this outcome?" if your mindset tells you your goals are unrealistic.

I am so passionate about creating a planning habit because I understand what it is like to be a distracted recruiter. I was a distracted recruiter when I first got into this business, and I struggled a lot when I opened. When I got my distractions under control through Focused Planning, finally, everything changed. Through Focused Planning, I made commitments to myself regarding the number of people I was going to talk to every day, the number of job orders I was going to take, and the number of interviews I needed to hit my financial goals. These commitments were just at a desk level, long before building my office. When you know your goals, you can get into a rhythm of knowing exactly how many people you need to talk to each day and week.

When you have full command of your Recruiter GPS, you can make a plan. Once you have a daily plan, you will see what you need to execute that plan. You may find that you need to have a list ready each day and to have that list requires outsourcing your research. Once you commit to the numbers, your deficits will become apparent. You can either choose to tackle them yourself or outsource some of them to a professional who is good at research, administrative work, et cetera.

Neglecting Focused Planning comes down to choosing not to plan when you do not have what you want. Choosing not to plan is choosing to continue to *not* have what you want in your recruiting business.

# FOCUSED PLANNING CASE STUDY

## DION BOWDEN – SEARCHRSA

Dion Bowden is the founder of Searchrsa based in Johannesburg, South Africa, and Atlanta, Georgia. Since 2001, Searchrsa has provided recruiting and staffing services to the actuarial, finance, chemical, mining, and manufacturing industries. Dion has also been a client of The RecruiterU since 2009 and is a coach in our Platinum and Boardroom programs.

## HOW HAVE YOU USED THE POWER OF FOCUSED PLANNING TO GROW YOUR FIRM?

Quite frankly, I do not know how you would grow your firm without planning it. The most important thing is to model the recruiting firm and understand how you are generating revenue and what activities you need to do to generate that revenue. And then, from that, your plan should come.

When talking to other recruiting firm owners, I have often seen them going down one avenue when their activity numbers are telling them they should be going down another. And that is because they are not looking at their overall metrics and business model and then using that as guidance for Focused Planning.

For me, Focused Planning starts with having a good understanding of your business and a good measure of your numbers and then using that as a way to scale your business.

If you need to build a million-dollar business, how many placements is that? How many first-time interviews? How many job orders? Well, if it means X number of job orders, do you have the correct number of marketing presentations available with your existing team in order to hit that? If it means X number of first-time interviews – and that means a certain number of submittals of candidates on your openings on a weekly basis – do you have enough recruiters to do those number of submittals?

From that master business model, everything cascades out in terms of how many recruiters you need, how many marketers you need, how many presentations to both prospects and candidates you need to be doing, and then how much research support you need on top of that. Focused Planning is imperative, and you will not hit large numbers without it.

## WHAT IS THE IMPORTANCE OF PLANNING FOR YOU AS THE FIRM OWNER AND YOUR TEAM?

For the firm owner, two things: One is to scale the business, and from what we just discussed previously, you definitely need to have a plan. The second part about planning as a firm owner and holding people accountable to a plan they have developed in cooperation with you removes the anxiety.

With Focused Planning, you are not going to need to beat people over the head to get them to work for you as a recruiter because then you hold them accountable to their own plans. These are billings and things that they said they wanted to achieve, and this is the plan that they need to execute on in order to achieve that goal. It reduces anxiety from a recruiting firm owner, gets you focusing on exactly what you need to focus on, and stops you from being one of those people that just manages by keeping people busy.

For a recruiter, it takes away the anxiety of what it is that you need to do on a daily and weekly basis in order to hit your revenue goal that you set for yourself. Instead of just coming in and working hard because that is what you need to do, you now come in and work smartly, and you know what it is that you need to achieve. If you are not achieving your billing goals and your activity goals, you can look at what is taking place and adjust the plan instead of waiting until the end of the year or the end of the month and seeing if you are hitting your billing numbers.

# PART 2: BECOMING A PURSUED PARTNER

## GOING FROM ANNOYING VENDOR TO TRUSTED ADVISOR

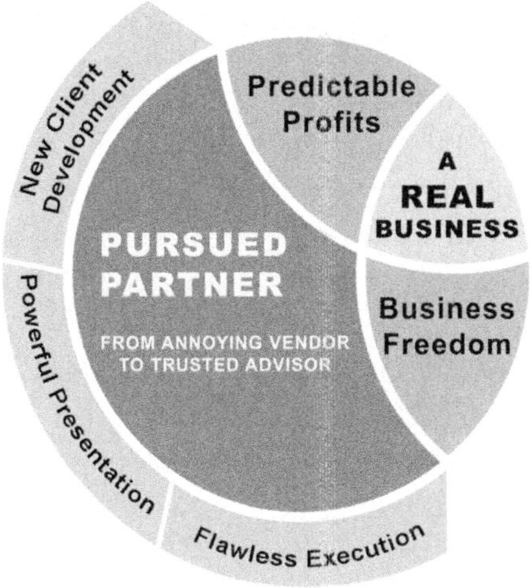

Many recruiters, especially tenured ones, have some clients who give them repeat business. A smaller subset of those have some *great* clients who work with them, respect their opinions, pay fair fees and even give them money upfront to conduct their searches.

For my first five or six years in the recruiting business, I worked primarily low fee, non-exclusive contingency assignments. It was *incredibly frustrating*! Clients were not getting back to me, they were filling the positions with alternate sources, et cetera. This way of recruiting was not the career I signed up for!

I made a *decision* to change the way I did business. I fired some bad clients and walked away from bad terms, and because of that, my business exploded in a good way! My business went from about $200,000 on my desk to over $1 million in less than three years. This opportunity is available to you.

Suppose one is consistently marketing, conducting a solid diagnostic backed by a Powerful Presentation, and finishing with a strong portfolio of candidates. In that case, you cannot help but have a group of amazing clients who retain you at outstanding fees on a long-term basis. I am your patron saint! I have done it both ways. Trust me, the latter is much preferred!

Pursued Partner is all about transitioning from being perceived by your clients as an annoying vendor to trusted advisor. There are three distinct components to making that transition. The first component is New Client Development or business development.

The second component is Powerful Presentation, which occurs once you engage a prospect or client on the phone. Powerful Presentation involves taking a great search assignment or job order.

The final component is Flawless Execution, which

involves everything that happens once you have the search. It is all about implementing the right recruiting campaign and having the right sourcing set up so that you blow your prospects away by presenting great talent to your clients and building a portfolio of clients aligned with your process.

# 7

# NEW CLIENT DEVELOPMENT

The first part of becoming a Pursued Partner by your clients is becoming strong in New Client Development, which is usually where most The RecruiterU clients struggle the most and where we have the most impact with them.

New Client Development, or new business development, is the hardest of the nine components of a *real* business. While some people have mastered it, many recruiters name this as their number one challenge. For the majority of the recruiting industry, this is the link where everything breaks down. I will only scratch the surface on the topic because this could be an entire book in and of itself.

## WHY RECRUITERS STRUGGLE WITH MARKETING AND NEW CLIENT DEVELOPMENT

The struggle with business development has nothing to do with a recruiter's ability, even though most recruiters believe it has everything to do with their ability. This is why we parallel mindset training and support with all of our clients and our programs. It is all about how you think about business development.

The problem is never the problem, especially in marketing. The problem is how one thinks about the problem of marketing. "What if I say the wrong thing?" "What if they do not need me?" When you pile all those beliefs on top of each other, you will feel anxious, and when you feel anxious, you procrastinate. That is why you go to LinkedIn to look for better candidates or exhaustively research a prospect by studying their web page before you even make a cold call only to get a voicemail or send an email that never gets returned.

In my experience, most recruiters do not struggle to make recruiting calls but struggle with marketing or new business development calls. Remember, there is one thing in common at the end of the call with both recruiting and marketing: a human being. You do not mind calling prospective candidates to recruit them, but you might have tons of excuses preventing you from calling a prospective client for marketing.

It is just that: people tell themselves false stories. The permanent placement business is estimated to be over $20 billion in revenue. It is not a fly-by-night industry but a well-respected industry with tremendous need. Companies use recruiters to fill positions that they cannot fill on their own. This happens *all the time!*

## BEST PRACTICES TO GENERATE MARKETING CONVERSATIONS

There is no one best mean of generating marketing conversations. The best approach is a combination that evolved from classic business development strategies and will continue to evolve. Over time, because everyone has gone to email and text, in clients who are measuring this, the return call rate on phone calls to voicemail is actually going up. It is not considered old school to pick up the phone and leave a message.

Be wary, though. The message you leave in a client's voicemail is crucial. Here is the message you do *not* want to leave: "Hi Mr./Ms. Prospective Client, I am checking in. I want to see if you need any help filling any positions." This voicemail will have the person on the other line hitting delete before hearing the remainder of your message.

When leaving a voicemail, immediately sending an email referencing your voicemail with a link to your calendar is a great best practice. This can be a simple template that you have ready to go that does not include a repeat of your voicemail but does include a link to your calendar to set up a call with you.

That email may say,

> "Hi Mr./ Ms. Prospective Client,
>
> "I just left you a message. Since we are both swamped, I wanted to share a link to my calendar so we can connect at a mutually convenient time for a quick chat."

The most effective way to generate marketing conversations, whether you're using voicemail, email, or text, is to add value to the prospect. Prospects have told us in focus groups year after year that they want to be kept abreast of great talent in the market. Even if they do not have an opening, they want to know about talent. If you contact someone with one prospect over several methods over days, a certain percent – 10 to 30 percent or higher – will get back to you.

Exposing your client base to top talent is one strategy that is still generating most of the new openings with new clients in our client base. Once the recruiter engages in an in-depth conversation, the client may or may not need that candidate.

If that's the case, you discover what they do need, positioning yourself to take a great search assignment.

## FLIP MARKETING

Another way our clients find success in generating marketing conversations is using a technique we call flip marketing. Flip marketing is when recruiters the recruiting call to recruit a hiring manager, then flip it into a marketing call. If you are talking to a prospective candidate that is not ready to make a move, flip the call by asking if they have any needs on their team or in their organization.

This savvy approach to transitioning the call from recruiting to marketing is a skill. We know most candidates are not looking when we approach them. The same is true for most hiring managers. I used a senior-level opening I worked on as a marketing vehicle for those who were not interested in my search. The key was working poor senior-level openings with low fees and non-exclusive terms with no real intent on filling them. Why? They are tremendous relationship building calls with future clients.

Developing this skill involves several hours of training that we provide all of our clients. Those who mastered this skill find that it yields a 30 to 40 percent return call rate.

## MARKETING A STAR CANDIDATE

There are some great ways to use technology to warm up your leads. One great use of technology is to create a short email that gives the impression that it is only going to that one person, not to a big list. This email is a quick, bullet-pointed profile of a candidate that highlights their successes without revealing the candidate's identity. This is a technique we call MPC (Most Placeable Candidate) email marketing.

These emails are *short* and highlight one or two of the candidate's *best* accomplishments that you know are in demand in your marketplace.

Here is an example.

> "Hi Mr./Ms. Hiring Manager,
>
> "In a recent engaged search, we uncovered a controller in the widget niche who reduced costs by $434,000 out of a $4 million budget in five and a half months while simultaneously increasing productivity by 12 percent on the financial team.
>
> "This individual is an expert at [A], [B], and [C] financially. [Describe these accomplishments in less than three sentences.]
>
> "Looking at your calendar, what is a good time to discuss this person's background in more detail?
>
> "Sincerely,
>
> "Joe/Jane Recruiter"

This marketing strategy involves a sequence of these emails sent out over the course of two to three weeks. This technique has a specific cadence and formula but results in generating marketing conversations with people ready to engage in your services.

## CONTENT MARKETING

Another means of passively warming people up is a longer-term strategy using content marketing. This is where consistency is paramount for generating results. Content marketing allows you to build credibility through the publication of educational content relevant to your clients' business. This is how I built my coaching business and how we help clients build their reputation, elevate themselves as thought leaders in their niche, and passively market to their entire database two to four times per month.

The beauty of this strategy is that your clients and prospects will start saying to themselves, "You know what? Those are my problems and issues. If this recruiter knows those are my problems or issues, maybe they can help me fix them."

When I teach this strategy to clients, the first question that always comes up is what to write about. Ask yourself these questions when planning your content: What are the most common problems or issues seen with our clients? What can you teach them? Some sample topics might include running better interview processes or making their offers more effective.

You might think sharing that content is giving away all of your secrets. The truth is that your clients and prospects are not going to completely implement any technique you share because there is always more to it. There is more expertise in the process that they do not possess. Sharing your techniques and insight will warm up your clients and prospects and allow them to respond in their own time.

Besides creating great content and remaining on the top of your prospects' mind with your entire database regularly, content marketing can generate marketing call lists through the reports generated by your email provider. You can use these reports to see who opened or clicked on a link in the email or which emails bounced and as the foundation of your weekly call lists.

The conversation can then focus on where the reader found value in the content and what types of topics they would like to read about in the future. Spoiler alert: the topics they share with you are most likely the pain points in their business.

## FAILING FORWARD IN MARKETING

I touched upon how the problem is not the problem but how you think about the problem. The real issue with marketing is the fear of rejection and a hypersensitivity to what someone who does not know you thinks about you. How are you supposed to stay motivated when you finally get that person on the phone and you keep hearing no?

I remember when I started the recruiting business. I was struggling. For those of you old enough to remember, in the late 1980s and early 1990s, Tony Robbins had a training series called *Personal Power*. I listened to the cassettes on my way to work. The message he gave resonated with me. He said, "The key for one to experience massive success is to experience massive failure." The amount of failure is directly correlated with the amount of success.

When you measure the metrics on cold calls, even in a good economy, it takes about thirteen actual conversations with a prospect (not email exchanges) to gain one search assignment or job order. Most people focus on the twelve noes. However, you need those twelve noes to lead to your one yes. As a motivation technique, I used to create little hand-drawn grids of fifteen boxes. I knew if I filled in the fifteen boxes with Xs, there would statistically be at least one yes.

Change your thinking about the fear of rejection by knowing that every no leads to the yes. You have to "fail" twelve times out of thirteen. Let's look at the failures in those marketing calls. Most, if not all, of the twelve noes sounded something like this:

• “No, we are not hiring right now.”

• “Thanks for calling. We just hired somebody.”

• “Thanks for calling. Call me in a month or two. We do not need anybody right now.”

Most of the twelve rejections or noes are actually, “No, not now.”

The rejections you face are benign. Whenever I ask, “How many of you get hung up on a lot?” on coaching calls or at any of our events, hands usually do not go up. In those rare instances where people have been hung up on, it is usually just a jerk on the other end of the phone. Even though getting hung up on is such a rare occurrence, people still have this fear around it.

When was the last time you got hung up on? If you have trouble remembering the last time or it was several months or years ago, is it rational to allow that rare event to drive your daily productivity?

Rejection is part of the process of recruiting. You are going to be rejected about 92 percent of the time. Each “rejection” gets you closer to your yes. For people who are motivated by money, you can even monetize each yes. Statistically, each yes is a job order, and your average fee is $20,000, and you place one out of four contingency openings. If it takes you thirteen conversations to get to the yes, each yes represents $5,000 (based on fulfilling one out of four contingency assignments). If each yes is $5,000, and you needed thirteen noes to get to your yes. Dividing thirteen into $5,000 is about $385 per no. Therefore, every time someone says no to you, you are actually cashing in $385. You need the twelve noes to get to the yes, which makes each no of equal value. Unless you're a mind reader, you need to go through the noes to get to the yes.

## THE PARADIGM OF BOTHER

There is a paradigm of bother that holds people back from successful marketing from a mindset and motivational standpoint. The root of this paradigm is a belief that sales are something you do to someone versus viewing sales as a service.

Sales are something you do *for* someone. If you think about the lives you changed and the companies you made more productive, you did everyone involved with a service through your placements. You have to successfully identify who wants that service, which is just part of the process. This means you may encounter many noes that are truly, "No, not now." Think of sales as something one is doing for someone, not something one is doing to someone.

The fear of bothering someone is ego-based. It assumes that you have so much power over others that your call will cause them distress. In reality, the person you are calling is always choosing. It is their choice to pick up the phone. It is also their choice to react in a certain way to your conversation. Bother is not something you do to another person. It is an emotion that that person feels in reaction to a situation. When you shift the paradigm to sales as a service, your entire viewpoint on marketing will change.

## FINAL THOUGHTS

New Client Development and marketing are all about consistency. The best time to market is when you have too many *good* openings. That is when you can afford to walk away from a bad search. You are busy with multiple searches, so you have more emotional power to reject any new bad ones. This is how I got more exclusives, higher fees, and more money upfront. I was negotiating from a position of strength, and you can too. You are never too busy to do business development, even if it is only for thirty minutes a day.

The worst strategy for marketing is getting a great non-exclusive or contingency opening, dropping everything you were doing to work on it, and then watching that search get filled through alternative means. When this occurs or you have nothing to work on, you feel like you have to settle for the next best available assignment.

When you market – and you do not have to market at the same pace – always do so for a minimum of half an hour to forty-five minutes a day, even if you have ten retained searches on your desk. You want to market a minimum of a half-hour a day because when somebody says, "We only pay 20 percent," or, "We have a six-month money-back guarantee," you are going to be in a much better position to negotiate better terms or walk away.

Think of marketing as a muscle. You need to train that muscle to keep it strong and toned consistently. When you skip too many workouts, it takes more effort and time to get your strength and endurance back.

Remember, the key to marketing to people you have never talked with before is to ask yourself these two main questions: "How do I add value to this cold conversation?" and "How does the prospect leave out interaction better off versus me just checking a box?" There are many different ways to do that, including introducing them to great talent, flip marketing, and content marketing.

Finally, look at how you think about marketing. Remember, the problem is never the problem. The problem is how you think about the business development problem.

# NEW CLIENT DEVELOPMENT CASE STUDY

## GERARD QUINLIVAN – CAMPBELL ROCHFORD

Gerard Quinlivan is a solo recruiter based in Dublin, Ireland. His executive search firm, Campbell Rochford, specializes in recruitment for the insurance industry in Ireland.

## HOW HAS YOUR NEW CLIENT DEVELOPMENT PROCESS CHANGED AND GROWN OVER TIME?

My process has changed enormously. Historically, my process was quite ad hoc and spontaneous and unstructured. I was never really a planner and never had a plan. I always approached New Client Development from a rather sporadic process in terms of developing new clients. I never came into the conversations with a plan, so a lot of what you would call my marketing approach would have been quite chaotic and unstructured for several years.

Since I joined The RecruiterU, I got really clear with myself and what my plan was around developing new clients specifically within my niche. I planned. I targeted specific clients whom I wanted to develop, that I wanted to work with, and that I saw as my client avatar.

That's probably the starting point, really, for me. It was developing a client avatar – the client that I really wanted to work with in the way that I wanted to work with them. I have seen that when you have a plan – not just in your head, but a plan written down that you can follow – you've got a structure, and with a structure, you have a routine that you can follow day by day.

Small changes made a big impact from a New Client Development perspective.

The biggest one probably was when I hired a researcher about eighteen months ago and started using that researcher to develop the brand and develop the client list a lot more than it had been. An example of that might be the fact that when I started that process. I probably had a network into maybe 200 brokers in Dublin – brokers who make up a big portion of my business. Now, I have a network from a client perspective, probably over 400 brokers. From a candidate recruit presentation perspective, I have a reach into thousands – I mean, multiples of multiples of candidates.

My marketing approach has very much changed from the point of view that it starts with a plan. It is very structured. I know who I need to reach, broadly what my plan is regarding who I am targeting, and what types of clients I want to be speaking with. And I think part of that is the MPC piece. MPCs were quite ad hoc and a sporadic thing for me. I would do one occasionally, but for me, it might be once every three or four months, which really wasn't an effective marketing strategy at all.

What I found in the last year and a half since I took on that researcher is that I now have a plan every week where I know that every Tuesday and every Thursday, I have to have my MPC prepared so that she can get those out to my mail list. She has been fantastic and has brought MailChimp into my life. She has introduced me to the concept of getting a mailing list together. We have a regular MPC that goes out twice a week, every week, and I make her hold me accountable for that.

Accountability is a big part as well as in the change in my approach. I hold myself accountable, but I also have my researcher hold me accountable. She will ping me every half an hour or every hour if I haven't sent her the MPC email by a certain time on a given day.

I was doing a little bit of content marketing as well. I have probably not done as much of that this year as I used to, undoubtedly because of the time required to do the content piece. And also because I felt that it probably was not getting as much traction from my clients on the content articles as much as the MPC articles. The MPC is probably the one marketing tool that I have adopted that really zeroes in on what you want your client to respond to. It zeroes in on and touches on the points that you want people reacting to, an example of which was on Friday evening just gone; I sent an MPC out at 5:00 p.m. on a Friday, which I know was probably not the "done" thing. Still, it was quite a targeted, focused MPC specific to a core group of clients who do not know more than twenty contacts in my sectors. By 5:30, I had two interviews organized for that candidate that week.

This success reinforced that for a long time – for several years – I was simply overlooking a key component of marketing and a key strategy that had been tremendously effective for me in terms of building clients and building my business.

## DID THIS APPROACH CHANGE YOUR CONFIDENCE WHEN DOING NEW CLIENT DEVELOPMENT AND MARKETING?

Yes, I think it has, but, indeed, I would not say it has necessarily changed my confidence. I think I was always pretty confident when I spoke to clients. But from a New Client Development perspective, it's a lot easier to go into a conversation with a new client and talk to them about a specific candidate if you have an MPC that you know will be of interest to them. You are inherently going to be a lot more confident going into that conversation because you have got something that you know is of value to the client. Historically, I probably would have gone into those calls with the tired questions: "Have you got any openings?" "What have you been doing recently?" "Tell me about your business."

It was more of a small thing that changed that view as well.

As I read *The Challenger Sale* by Matthew Dixon and Brent Adamson, it totally resonated with me because I realized that for many years, I have always been a relationship-driven salesperson, with sales built on the back of very, very solid relationships with clients I've known for a long time, which is good. After all, it does generate repeat business. Still, it was not really driving new business or New Client Development because I was not forcing myself into those conversations where I had to speak to someone I had never spoken with before.

I think an MPC is a hugely advantageous tool to allow you to open up the conversation with a new client because you can go into that conversation confident that you have something of value to offer them. I'm pretty confident that even if the candidate or that individual is not a fit for them there and then, a follow-up conversation will come off the back of that. Now, I view the MPCs as a conduit very much to a conversation. I don't expect them to generate interviews every time I send them out necessarily. I see them more as a conduit to a conversation with a new client or with a client I might not have spoken to for quite a long time.

## HOW HAS ALL OF THIS IMPACTED YOUR RECRUITMENT PRACTICE?

In straightforward terms, the metrics are probably the one thing that I can point to as evidence of how it has impacted my business. I will give you some specific examples. In 2020, both pre- and post-lockdown due to the pandemic, my total billings for the entire year comprised no more than about €25,000, which is roughly $32,000. In 2021, year-to-date, the first quarter is not quite over yet; I am currently on €74,500. I initially set out a target for the year of billing over €200,000 euro, and on the run rate I am on at the moment, I am heading now for €330,000.

If you take that as a measurement of where I was and where I am now, I've gone from €25,000 to €330,000 in terms of my expectations. That has been probably the most impactful piece for me – the metrics. I cannot point to any one MPC email or marketing effort or initiative I undertook as the game-changer. I do not think it was any one thing. I think it was a lot of series of very small things that contributed to all of that.

## IS THERE ANYTHING ELSE THAT YOU WANT TO SHARE ABOUT NEW CLIENT DEVELOPMENT?

I think it is really important that you have a plan. I think planning can be underestimated. As I said at the outset, I think for too long, I was unstructured and unfocused. I was kind of happy-go-lucky about it. Invariably, new clients would come along occasionally, but because I did not have a plan or a focus around what those new clients might look like, invariably, what I was doing was picking up contingency orders and openings with clients who I subsequently found I did not particularly like working with or I did not particularly want to work with. "Ah, sure, I'll pick up a new client when I need them."

I think for me, a hugely powerful tool that I picked up from The RecruiterU is the ability to say no to stuff that historically I would have said yes to. I am able to walk away from it. I think it is as important for your business to know who the right clients are to work with certainly. Equally important is to know which clients you want to walk away from and not invest your time in. I could easily spend twenty or thirty hours wasted on a search on behalf of a contingency client that I would be frustrated with at the end of it. I would say, "Well, that was a waste of my time," and it would give me lots of reasons not to do New Client Development because, in my mind, I would be thinking, "Well, I did that. I did not work out. I wasted a lot of time, and I got zip for it." Whereas I go through the diagnostic or maybe invest an hour with a new client. If I conclude at the end of that diagnostic that this is not the right opening or the right opening to work from my perspective, I respectfully pass. I explain to the client that, unfortunately, there is a disconnect. That, as much as anything else, has saved me a tremendous amount of time and energy because I know now I can identify pretty quickly from those diagnostic conversations, particularly with new clients, whether or not this is a client that I want to invest my time with.

Note: “diagnostic” is the term we use at The RecruiterU that relates to the process of taking a new search assignment in a highly consultative way.

# 8

# POWERFUL PRESENTATION

You are continuing your journey through the Pursued Partner section of the Recruiting Firm Optimizer Model, which is transitioning from an annoying vendor to a trusted advisor. Now you successfully have somebody on the phone with a need who is ready to engage in your services. This is where most recruiters put themselves into the commodity zone.

## COMMON PITFALLS OF TAKING JOB ORDERS OR SEARCH ASSIGNMENTS

Traditional recruiter training does a disservice to the profession. It is the reason most recruiters land in the commodity zone. This is not your fault; as in all professions, how you approach your work evolves. Recruiting, in many ways, is still stuck in the past, which is why I am so passionate about helping tenured and newer solo recruiters and recruiting firm owners to learn new techniques that elevate their status with their clients to trusted advisors.

Most recruiters were taught to ask these five basic questions when taking a search:

- What are you looking for?

- What background is required?

- What are the duties and responsibilities?

- What is the compensation package?

- If you found the right candidate, could you pay him or her a little more to get them on board?

There is nothing wrong with these questions; it is just that every other recruiter hiring managers are speaking to is asking the same questions.

Most recruiters mess up at this stage because they ask typical questions all recruiters ask, and they allow the client to take control of the call to dictate the timing and responses. Most recruiters are not adept at challenging answers they get from the hiring managers, even if they know that in the marketplace, either that person does not exist in the right quantity or that person does not exist at that compensation number. In the end, most recruiters end up being order takers, not search consultants.

How do you differentiate yourself from everyone else in the recruiting industry? By presenting yourself differently. Instead of asking the questions every other recruiter asks, ask highly consultative questions. These questions allow you to gather much better and deeper information than the usual questions. Because they sound different, the hiring manager will view you differently from other recruiters. When somebody says they have an opening, you transition into performing a great diagnosis.

## CRAFTING A POWERFUL PRESENTATION

> *"A prescription without a diagnosis is recruiting malpractice."*
>
> — ROB MOSELY

We often get asked how to "pitch" a retainer. The short answer is, you don't. Baseballs are for pitching. Retainers, engaged searches, and exclusives are sold through a highly consultative process. The key to getting retainers is changing all the questions in your search assignment and performing a phenomenal diagnosis to uncover the pain. This involves asking specific questions that reveal the true problem to discover the consequences for leaving the position open and to uncover the weekly pains the hiring manger experiences when the position remains vacant.

When I am doing a presentation to a group of recruiting firm owners, I always ask, "If someone agrees to give you money upfront on an assignment, what did they do?"

The responses I usually hear are:

- "They bought your expertise."
- "They bought your time."
- "They bought you as a professional."

Yes, expertise and time are true, but they are not *the* reason people pay retainers. The reason people pay retainers is because the client can surmise that this recruiter will fill the position. The client is buying a filled position. How do they buy a filled position? With the process you take them through.

A prescription without diagnosis means the information gathered is surface level – the client needs somebody with three to five years to do these things at this compensation level. That is not a great diagnosis. At The RecruiterU, we teach every one of our clients how to perform a phenomenal diagnosis. A phenomenal diagnostic question is one like this:

"Imagine this person started a year from now, and they have had an outstanding first year. What did he or she accomplish?"

Ask this question instead of the standard, "What are the duties and responsibilities?" Another question many recruiters ask is, "What is the background you are looking for?" If you are going to be a true trusted advisor, you need to uncover the problem you are trying to solve *first*.

The first question gave you insight into what a great first year looks like. From there, you can ask this alternative to the "what is the background you are looking for" question:

"Based on your level of expertise, Mr./Ms. Hiring Manager, what has to already be in place? What are the critical success factors they need to have to meet that standard in your organization?"

As you can see, this the same type of question only asked much differently. When you ask the question this way, you will get richer responses because it requires the person to imagine. When they imagine, they actually go to the visual part of their brain and create an image.

Finally, another critical question to ask is, "What are the consequences of the position remaining open?" In the absence of the client having any frustration or pain, they will be reluctant to pay you money upfront or give you an exclusive.

The first stage to selling retained or exclusive search is diagnosis. Once you clearly define what the hiring manager is looking for and what a great first year looks like and outlined compensation, benefits, and selling points of the opportunity, you complete the process of taking the search.

Next is the prescription phase, where you explain, in explicit detail, what you are going to do to fill the position. You walk them through, step by detailed step, what exactly you are going to do to fill the position. For example, you can share that based on the requirements of the type of candidates they are looking for, your research team (even if you are a solo recruiter) will put together a list of 60, 80, or 100 individuals. The size of the list will be dependent upon the niche the candidates come from.

Explain that you will attempt to have a conversation with each individual up to seven times over the next thirty days. If you have not successfully spoken with someone by the seventh attempt, that is a clear indicator that they are not interested in making a career move. Impress upon the client that you will talk to several interested candidates who are either qualified or unqualified. Through this process, you will identify three or four candidates, and if you have done your job properly, the decision on which one to hire will be challenging.

You can go into even more detail, but this is the framework for doing a phenomenal diagnosis and thorough prescription. Once you do this, the only thing left to do is quote the fee. This is how I frame this last part of the process: "For us to engage in the process I just described represents an investment of 28.6 percent of the individual's first-year base salary, and for us to do that, that is a $5,000 upfront deposit, which is fully credited on the backend."

That is the process for selling retained search. The formula is simple: Perform a phenomenal diagnostic through questions that distinguish yourself from every other recruiter but still allow you to gather the necessary information. Once you complete your diagnosis, provide a detailed prescription of how you will find your client's best talent. Finally, share the investment needed by the client for you to make this all happen.

## HOW TO NAVIGATE FEE NEGOTIATIONS

Once you go through this process and quote the fee, the client will most likely want to negotiate your fee. This is perfectly normal; clients always want to negotiate; it makes them good businesspeople. Fee negotiation is an art that deserves much more than a few paragraphs, but you can decide what points of negotiation you wish to concede to or dig your heels about. One of the easiest areas to negotiate is the deposit; you may lower the deposit to a $3,500 deposit instead of a $5,000 deposit. That is a business decision that only you can make.

However, your client may counter that all the other recruiters they have spoken to have agreed to do this for 20 percent on contingency. This is where I always ask the simple question, "So, why are we talking?" When I ask this, I go quiet. Most of the time, the response is, "They are not doing the job." Exactly!

When the client wants to negotiate the terms of the fee, this is another opportunity to position yourself as different from every other recruiter and to position yourself as a trusted advisor. Fee negotiation is where other recruiters fail because they do not reiterate to the client the consequences for the position remaining open. That statement may sound similar to this:

> "You just said, Mr./Ms. Employer, if you do not have this person on in the next thirty days, they will miss your company-wide meeting, or they are going to miss your product launch, which would cost you a lot of money. Again, is it that important? Can you leave it to chance?"

When it came down to companies wanting to negotiate on a retainer, I was not successful 100 percent of the time when having these conversations. I was successful about a third of the time. However, the placement ratios for retained business trend more toward nine out of ten positions successfully filled versus contingency at one in four or five. I let some business walk away if the client and I could not come to a mutually beneficial agreement.

The key in the negotiation process is that you performed a fantastic diagnosis. Ask excellent questions and have a complete understanding of why the position remains open. With this information, clearly articulate back to the client the cost of that position remaining open.

## IS THERE EVER A PLACE FOR CONTINGENCY ASSIGNMENTS?

While exclusives, deposit-based searches, and retainers are ideal, most of the permanent placement business is contingency. I am not saying to not take contingency. Many recruiting firms realized success in making contingency placements. In my own firm, there was a blend of retained, exclusive, and contingency assignments. I see this same dynamic with my coaching clients.

The process of diagnosis and prescription used for selling

retainers is applicable for all types of searches. The beauty of this process is that when you take them through it, even if you are a full contingent recruiter, it increases the likelihood of you gaining an exclusive. Let's say you are not yet comfortable with retainers. You can say, "For us to do this, I need a thirty-day or a forty-five-day exclusive where you do not hire any other recruiter."

This process will also help you raise your fees because you can now have a higher contingency fee with a great diagnosis and prescription. My preference was to migrate my desk from fully contingent to 90 percent retained in my business. As my firm grew and added new recruiters, most of my recruiters were doing about a fifty-fifty split of retained and contingent.

When you look at contingency, the contingent assignments you want to work on are ones where you have access to the hiring manager or, at minimum, a strong feedback loop with human resources and timeliness in their process. You want to receive feedback at all stages: from submitting a resume to the first interview, from the first interview to the second interview, and from the second or last interview to offer.

The type of contingency I recommend you never work are search assignments where you submit candidate resumes through a portal and the client gets back to you in a month after they hired the person. Done the right way, however, contingency is good business.

### *Making the Transition from Contingency to Retained Search*

People ask me how they can transition current clients from contingency to retained search all the time. You might have clients who you work with on contingency where you fill most of the openings. That being the case, I would not try to migrate them because there is minimal benefit to you, and you might risk harming that relationship.

However, if you have a client that constantly gives you openings, but you only can fill one in three or four assignments because they are working with other recruiters or canceled the search for a variety of reasons, you can go back and have the same conversation you would with a new client. I go back to that client and do a great diagnosis, followed by a fantastic prescription, and then explain to them that I have a new way of approaching my business.

You can say to them,

> "We are changing the way we are doing our business. We are adding even more value. This means we will invest more in your searches by adding more research to uncover a larger pool of candidates. We are going to make seven attempts to reach each of those candidates in order to present to three or four that would be a great fit for your position. This is not a level of support that I could provide on contingency assignments. Mr./Ms. Hiring Manager, you already know me. You know I have placed a few of your team members, who are doing great. Those candidates were found with one hand tied behind my back. After all, I could not fully implement this process because I knew you had other recruiters working on this assignment. I want to change that for both you and me."

The same language is used as if you were to sell retained search to a new client.

As with selling retainers to a new client, the key here is to ensure that the recruiter did the work to uncover the consequences of the position remaining open. It is this knowledge that I capitalize on, especially with someone I have already worked with, when they inevitably say, "We don't want to pay money upfront." This is especially common with somebody that already worked with you.

My response, when asked this question, is to bluntly say,

> "Do you think I won't fill the position? Because, again, we have already placed a couple of people with you. My fear is I know I have worked on things, and honestly, you filled them through alternative means, or you canceled them, and we lost a ton of money doing research. I cannot afford to do that anymore, but I do want to provide more value. Again, I will keep the fee the same. All I am asking is for $5,000 of that fee upfront. Our average fee has been $20,000. I am going to take that off at the end. You send me $5,000 now, and you will send me $15,000 later. I can see that you would not be willing to do that if you do not think I will fill the position. Maybe that is a different conversation that you would like to have."

As mentioned before, if you have great contingency clients with whom you can fill eight or nine out of ten openings, you do not have to transition them to retained clients. It is the promiscuous client who uses you like a free research firm that you want to have that discussion with.

## FINAL THOUGHTS

The key to Powerful Presentation is becoming a trusted advisor by distinguishing yourself from every other recruiter. I like to recommend a book called *The Challenger Sale* by Matthew Dixon and Brent Adamson if you need to hone your sales skills. The book is based on the authors' study of several thousand sales representatives and sales managers. This study showed that those with the most effective sales approach possessed what they call the Challenger Sales personality. Someone with a challenger sales personality understands their client's business and is willing to challenge the norms of that client's business.

That is the type of recruiter most of your clients want: somebody that understands their business and will challenge their approach and their way of doing business. When you do those things, combined with a great diagnostic and prescription process, you significantly increase the likelihood of not only getting retainers but gaining and retaining great clients.

# POWERFUL PRESENTATION CASE STUDY

## JEFF KING – RQ FOCUS

Jeff King is the Founder of RQ Focus, a solo recruiting practice specializing in the life sciences industry located in the San Francisco Bay area. Jeff's practice is a highly defined niche because he only works with regulatory and quality professionals for life sciences companies in the San Francisco Bay area.

## WHAT DOES "POWERFUL PRESENTATION" MEAN TO YOU?

To me, Powerful Presentation means understanding what your client needs – not just telling them what you think you can do for them but finding out what it is that they really need. One of the things that I have learned, too, is by digging in a little bit more as to what is the underlying purpose for this need, you find out a lot more and find out how this need affects the hiring manager directly finding out their story. Like, what are they suffering through as well? It helps you define the urgency a little bit more. And I think it is also taking the time to learn a little bit more about the solution that they think they need because sometimes, what they think they need can be limiting them.

The hiring manager may be looking for too many things. I am finding out the need and digging down to the core of the solution for them. This process is more consultative instead of just being more transactional, just finding out a little more about what they are looking for, and then helping them determine the best way to move forward.

## HOW DO YOU DIG IN AND HELP YOUR CLIENTS DETERMINE THE BEST WAY TO MOVE FORWARD?

I just ask a lot of good questions, such as:

- "Why is this position open?"

- "How is this affecting you on a daily basis?"

- "What do you see as being a good solution for this?"

- "What is it that you are looking for?"

- "What can you live with, and what can you not live without?"

Just kind of digging into those things. And then you get a chance to talk a bit about yourself once you have identified a little bit more of what they are looking for. Asking these questions is your chance to help set yourself apart from other recruiters that they may be talking to as well. It also allows you to lay out what your plan is.

One of the things that I found by doing this a little bit more is that people are shocked by how much work goes into recruiting. So many of my prospects and clients think recruiting is an easy thing. They believe I have all these resumes and just send them on over. By digging into their business and talking with them in detail about our process that The RecruiterU taught me – "I will make this many attempts with this many people" – they realize that you are making hundreds of phone calls and sending emails and all that to people to try to fill their position. Most clients have no idea, so this conversation starts to help set you apart as well too.

From here, I even go a step further and get their input as to how to sell this opportunity. What is the messaging that we can take out to people that are probably not looking for jobs – the ones that are really doing very well in their job? It helps set you up as a little bit more of a consultant instead of just someone who will post a job right next to theirs that is for the same thing and then see the same people they would be seeing. That gives them a little bit more buy-in too.

I think Powerful Presentation is just going to a state of being more of a consultant with them. It lets them know what is going to happen, sets expectations, and just lets them know what I do, and then asking them the question, "Have you experienced that with other recruiters in the past?" Most of the time, they say, "No, I have not had anything like this before." That alone already starts setting you apart and giving you a little bit more credibility because you are not just doing the same thing that they are used to. You are getting them more involved in the process and getting their buy-in a little bit more as you go along too.

Powerful Presentation is in the client's best interests because you are finding out really what they need. But it is in your best interest too because it helps set you apart once it starts coming down to negotiating the fee.

I have had so much less resistance about the fee now because the client thinks, "I will not even try to talk you down because you are doing all these things in your search process." If you let them know what their dollars are getting, they are more willing to say, "Yeah, let's do that."

I will ask them after I lay out my plan; I will just ask if that sounds like something they are familiar with? Is that something that you think might be better than what you have done in the past? Most of the time, they say, "Yes, it is, it is a lot better than what we are doing." I will let them know, "Well, I might not be the cheapest, but at least you have an idea of what I will be doing."

Then, from there, we may start talking about the negotiations for the contract. It has been really surprising. By taking this approach, I give them an idea of my rate; it is a little bit different for each role because each role has different nuances. In some cases, I will just say, "I am not sure I can help you out on this one." They are surprised by the honesty, or they will say that they have concerns about dealing exclusive or something like that. I will let them know that I cannot do that on a contingent basis because of all of the steps that I have outlined that I will do for this.

I explain that if we are bringing in all these other contingencies, this other stuff will take time to get the detail you are looking for. "If I am trying to beat somebody else by getting a date stamp on a resume in there quicker to you, I have got to cut all of that out, or at least a large portion of it." Then, I ask if they want me to cut that out. They usually do not want me to do so. Then, it makes the discussion about retainers and exclusives so much easier.

It is just a matter of getting them to be on the exclusive timeframe or the upfront money, but that is not a discussion that I fear anymore. Actually, I like it. If the client says that they can only do contingency or asks what to do about these other agencies in there working on it, I'll just say, "Unfortunately, I am going to have to step away from that one. I have to prioritize my work as well to my other clients who are doing exclusives and retained."

It has been surprising. When I have done that – certainly not all the time, but a number of times –they have come back and said, "What if we have the other recruiter stop working on it and then give you some money upfront?" That is something that I did not think was going to happen. I just thought they would say, "Okay, fine, we will do what we are doing." But I have had a few of them say, "No, we want what you described. We want that process that you described that we feel is going to give us a better outcome."

Powerful Presentation has made many clients willing to come back either put a little bit of money upfront or make it exclusive, get rid of the other recruiters, and sign an exclusivity agreement.

I think doing this kind of presentation and letting them know what they will be getting has made the contract negotiations so much simpler. It does not become an issue because now I am not a commodity. Now, they are hiring a consultant.

## HOW HAS THAT SHIFT FROM CONTINGENCY TO MORE EXCLUSIVE AND RETAINED CHANGED YOUR BUSINESS, YOUR OUTLOOK, AND HOW YOU WORK?

Moving from contingency to exclusive and retained has changed everything. I was chasing all that contingency work for years, and you would bust your butt trying to get things done. You would be just a little bit too late with getting a resume in there for someone that ultimately got hired. Or you chase after people for quite a while and do not get anything for it, and you realize that you wasted so much time and feel that you should have never taken that search.

I think that is the thing, too, as I have gotten better at saying no, I enjoy saying no more now. I have said no to three clients in the last month after having them go through what their needs were, finding out what they think they need, determining what the solution might be, and finding out the gaps between what the required skills are and what they are willing to pay for it. And if there are any red flags revealed in the conversation, this might be something that I do not want to take as retained or even exclusive. After all, it's not going to get billed more than likely, and then, having to have those conversations with them, they are not as competitive.

I think that is one of the things with the clients who I have been taking on as retained or exclusive, where I am that consultant again, is that I can go back to them and share with them the issues I am having as I am going out and talking with people. The candidate might already be at X amount of dollars right now, so what you are offering will be more of a lateral move. I can explain that we will have a hard time getting people to make a lateral move.

The beauty of Powerful Presentation is that I can talk to and work with the client and say, "Let's go back and re-approach this," based on what I learn from the candidate marketplace. If I am on a contingency, I am not going to do that; I will let the client know that I am going to drop the search. When I have worked contingency before, that is exactly how I would work, so if they are seeing a contingency recruiter is working for them, and then suddenly, they see all the activity drop off, that might be what is going on. They are just not hearing about it because there is no skin in the game for either side.

Powerful Presentation has made my days much more efficient and enjoyable. I am having completely different conversations with completely different people now than I was two years ago. I have been working with The RecruiterU since March 2020 and have been having better conversations the longer I am in the program.

Before, I was having conversations with internal recruiters and human resources and people like that about, "What is your fee?" Now, I am talking more to VPs, cofounders, and CEOs of companies and talking more about an overall plan for their recruiting as the company is growing. I have better conversations with people who can make the decisions, and I am just treated completely differently. My phone calls are taken. A lot of times, when I am working with HR right now, that is going to be an HR partner who is actually helping me instead of me just talking to them.

Powerful Presentation has made a huge difference in the enjoyment of the job. It has made a huge difference in my productivity and also in the outcome for the clients. I am filling a lot more of the positions now instead of beating my head against the wall and doing contingency work. If the search assignment is not retained, even just getting an exclusive – just something from them that says they are valuing my time and the effort – I will put into the search for them. That has made a huge difference.

Learning how to execute the concept of Powerful Presentation effectively has made me up my game as I was talking to prospective clients. I had always tried to deliver on the recruiting side, even when I was doing the contingency work, but I always felt like, "Jeff, you are doing retained work at a contingency price and sometimes not even get paid for it." I felt cheated, but it was my own fault for not asking for the exclusive or the retained. Now that I am letting people know the effort that I am putting into it, it is a lot easier to get that level of commitment from them as well. It has made me up my game all the way around. I feel more like a consultant than a telemarketer trying to sell resumes.

There have been some fumbles along the way as I got better at it. There still are. As I do some of these presentations, I am still learning things. I am still learning how I should approach exclusives and things like that. It is an ongoing process, but I am getting better at it. I am getting much more comfortable with it, and I enjoy the work a lot better from doing it that way.

# 9

# FLAWLESS EXECUTION

Flawless Execution is a search done so well that it provides a phenomenal portfolio of candidates to your clients, one from which your client struggles to determine which candidate they should hire. A lot of times, what you hear if you have done an incredibly fantastic job on a search is, "I could hire two or three of these." That is the essence of Flawless Execution: providing your clients with a portfolio of outstanding talent.

Flawless Execution is essential, especially in a strong market, to becoming a trusted advisor to your clients. If the top candidate turns down the job offer, you already have a solid backup. One of the biggest mistakes I see many recruiters make is that they stop recruiting when they have a candidate that they think the client will extend an offer to, and even if the client makes the offer, something happens, and the deal does not come together. Without a strong backup, the recruiter is starting, essentially, from scratch. When you have flawlessly executed, you immediately have one, two, or even three great alternative candidates to present to your client.

There are three other common mistakes recruiters when executing on a search assignment besides stopping recruiting candidates too soon.

## MISTAKE 1: LACKING A STRATEGIC SEARCH PLAN OR ANY PLAN AT ALL

It is easy to dive headfirst into a new search as soon as you hang up with the client. There is a certain excitement to having a new search to work on; something new is always exciting. Instead of creating a strategic plan for the search, the first thing recruiters tend to do is a database or LinkedIn search looking for candidates that match the assignment.

Dropping everything to work on a new search without a plan is like buying wood, appliances, and sheet rock for your new house before the architectural plan is ready.

## MISTAKE 2: DOING YOUR RESEARCH ON YOUR OWN TO SAVE MONEY OR EFFORT

There is a common misconception that outsourcing research is expensive. There is also a misconception, usually rooted in ego, that nobody can do research as well as you. In addition, there is the belief that an outsourced research professional is not capable of finding the information you are seeking.

The vast majority of recruiters we work with at The RecruiterU originally felt the same way. They felt that they could find great candidates (and clients) on their own by searching LinkedIn and Google. They spent countless hours developing boolean search strings to build a list.

The truth is – and what they learned is – these recruiters are performing a $10-an-hour activity when their time is worth $150 to $300 an hour. What they *really* learned was that doing their own research cost them $140 to $290 per hour!

## MISTAKE 3: PITCHING JOBS TO CANDIDATES

I used that word "pitch" on purpose. As I said before, pitching is for baseballs. When it comes to recruiting great talent, you need first to understand that person's specific needs. You need to understand their career ambitions and where the gap lies between their current role and their career ambition.

Recruiting talent for your clients is the same process as marketing to potential clients. It requires performing a phenomenal diagnostic by asking questions to help gauge where that person is in their career and how serious they are about making a change. Not asking great questions makes you sound like every other recruiter out there and puts you directly into the commodity zone.

## STRATEGIES FOR FINDING PASSIVE TALENT

We know passive talent is really what clients want, but what is the best way to find passive talent? Finding passive talent is truly a numbers game. You need to talk to numerous people to find the best available person on the market. The promise I make our clients and the promise we recommend to our clients, recruiting firm owners and solo operators alike, is that you will find the best available person in the marketplace – the keywords being "the best available." The promise is not necessarily to deliver the best person in the marketplace because the best person may be unavailable right now. The best person might have just received a significant raise or is awaiting a big bonus outstanding. However, the best available person is ready for a career change now.

Finding the best available person in the market is both having a great process and engaging with many candidates. Again, the best way to find passive talent is to hire a researcher to compile a great list of potential people for you to contact. You want to have at least fifty people on that list. The only exception is if you are looking for a unique individual, such as a left-handed nuclear engineer that has to be based in El Paso, Texas, because the company is not open to relocation. Every search plan should have fifty to one-hundred names and contacts on them.

I cannot emphasize this enough: putting together that list is the role of the researcher. Yes, some of those people might also be in your database. Still, a research professional will uncover many more potential candidates that are not already in your database.

Once you have your list, implement the same process you outline to your client when securing the search. Over the course of three weeks, make five to seven attempts to have a conversation with each candidate before you abandon talking to them. Most, not all, passive candidates will not respond after the first or second attempt. (This, by the way, is when *most* recruiters give up!) The person who actively is searching for a job will usually get right back to you.

I cannot tell you how many times we have this argument with our recruiting firm owner clients. They challenge me by saying, "There is no way I am going make seven attempts with each person on my list." I have testimonials from clients who tried recruiting candidates my way. They made $50,000 to $60,000 placements on the sixth or seventh attempt to a candidate. It was at this attempt where the candidate actually *apologized* for not getting back to them.

What is the definition of an attempt? An attempt is a combination of voicemails, emails, InMails, and text messages. These attempts are not going to be seven voicemails left in seven days. You might leave a voicemail and then send a quick follow-up email. That email can read:

> "Hey Candidate, I just left you a message. I have no idea what is going on in your career. I just wanted to have a quick conversation to see if you are open to hearing about something potentially stronger than your current situation. You can reach me at [phone number]."

You can mix up the messaging a little bit with each attempt. For example, if you spoke with this candidate in the past, you might say on a voicemail, email, or text:

> "Hi Candidate. You said if I ran across a mid-sized company that did this, this, and this, to let you know. I think I found something like that. You can reach me at [phone number]."

You could even give them one teaser of the position. Again, the same verbiage could be left in voicemail, email, or text.

On the seventh and last attempt, I would always leave this disengagement message:

> "Hey Candidate, I left you several messages over the last couple of weeks. If I do not hear back from you by the close of business today, I will assume you no longer want to hear about opportunities in your profession, and we will take you off our list. If I am mistaken, please get a hold of me at this phone number."

That last call actually has the highest return rate. Most people say that this message is bold. I had coaching clients question if the candidates would be upset when receiving it. My experience with using this disengagement message is, no, the candidate is not upset at all. They are apologetic. The candidates you get in those conversations are some of the best candidates you work with.

One of the advantages of this process is most of your competitors are giving up after one, two, or three attempts, and most of the best talent is available when you contact them on the fourth attempt or later. Several studies – both formal and my own informal studies within my recruiting firm and with coaching clients– on cold and warm calling, not only for talking to candidates but also in selling your services, show that you are likely to reach 90 percent of the people on your list after the sixth attempt. After two attempts, the likelihood is less than 20 percent. Persistence is a technique that most of your competition is not employing, which works to your advantage!

Now that you have a list of the best available people in the market, the step is to engage those highly sought-after passive candidates. When they woke up that morning, they probably were not thinking, *"I need to get a new job,"* or, *"I want to restart my career."* We all know that there is no such thing as a perfect company or a perfect opportunity. When you get the candidate on the phone, it is crucial not to fall into the trap of "pitching the job" to them. Instead, you want to get curious about their current position and how it aligns with where they want to go in their career.

That conversation may sound something like this:

> "Hey, you know Mr./Ms. Candidate, I know there is no such thing as a perfect company or a perfect opportunity, but if you had to describe some of those minor imperfections in your current role with your current company, what would some of those be?"

This type of questioning brings them inward and encourages them to think about things, problems, et cetera that are irritating them in their current role. The passive candidate is thinking about these things every day, but because most passive candidates are not miserable (they only experience *some* unhappiness), they are not pursuing a change.

To effectively engage a passive candidate, determine if those small areas of discomfort are in alignment with what your client is providing. Ask questions that get them focused on what irritates them. If you are an experienced recruiter, how many times have you spoke to someone and in the first conversation they were "open" to making a move and a month later they want *out* of their job? Why does that happen? When they focus on what irritates them in their position, they see *more* of what irritates them!

## STRATEGIES TO USE RECRUITING CALLS FOR BUSINESS DEVELOPMENT

When speaking to passive candidates and diving into the imperfections of their current organization, you may notice the candidate feels that everything is perfect. The truth is that some people are thrilled in their position. If somebody said, "Things are going fantastic," I always congratulate them on that. "Awesome, congratulations. Tell me about the things that you love doing." I flip the conversation into why they love it there.

Why do I do that? First, I want to know if this is an excellent opportunity to find a new client based on my conversation. Second, sometimes in the course of the conversation, the candidate may drift to an area of imperfection and irritation in their current role. When engaging in this type of conversation, listen more than you speak. I am always mindful of speaking 15 to 20 percent of the time and listen the remaining 80 percent.

During a search, there will times where you will talk to three or four people who absolutely love where they work. I use this as a marketing opportunity and called the candidate's manager. For example, if I were to call the VP of operations, the voicemail I leave might be,

> "Hey Mr./Ms. VP, I talked to several people in your organization, and I have some interesting information for you. I just thought you might like to know. You can reach me at [phone number]."

That voicemail message has a 98 percent return call rate. When they call back, the conversation usually goes something like,

> "I just figured in today's business environment, there is a lot of stress and pressure. I will not give out any names, but I talked to a couple of your team members, and they love it there. They absolutely love it there, and here is why they love it. [I then give some specific reasons.] My call here, Mr./Ms. VP, is not entirely altruistic. I want to ask you, what do I need to do to earn the right to help you build your team? I want to find people to put them into that type of culture and environment."

Sometimes, you will get a client out of that conversation. You can use a recruiting call with a candidate who is happy at their current organization and turn it into future business development.

## NAVIGATING THE OFFER NEGOTIATION PROCESS

The negotiation process begins with your initial conversation with the candidate. During that initial call, it is imperative to be crystal clear about the candidate's needs. Most recruiters get stung by candidates at the offer stage because they are loose in their questions on their early calls with the candidate. Before an interview ever takes place, go through this process with the candidate. You and the candidate need to be clear on the following:

- What do they need benefits-wise?
- What do they need time-off-wise?
- What do they need travel-wise?
- What do they need financially?
- What are the tradeoffs?
- If you find something you absolutely love (and what does that look like?), is the money flexible?
- What is the lowest salary number at which you would walk away?

Throughout the interview process, check-in with the candidate.

For example, imagine a candidate is interviewing for a position with a $100,000 salary, and the person is currently at $95,000. The client's range is $90,000 to $110,000, but we all know that companies rarely pay the high end of the range.

Depending on the opportunity, candidates are not going to take a cut in salary.

The second key to successful offer negotiations is never to share the range with the candidate. Never tell a candidate who is at $95,000 that the range for the position they are interviewing for is $90,000 to $110,000. The only number they will hear is $110,000.

Instead, ask if the candidate would be open to a lateral move for the right opportunity. Do not get hung up on whether it is yes or no. You just want to understand where their thinking is. One of the most common mistakes I see recruiters having this conversation with a candidate too late in the process. My question to the candidate is always, "What is the number you would need at a minimum?" As the process goes on, if the client is looking to pay around $95,000, I tell the client to back off and move on with another candidate.

The best way to handle the entire interview and negotiation process is to check in after every stage of the interview process. Before the first interview, the candidate might say that they will make a lateral move for the right opportunity but would need at least $102,000 to make a change. That is a reasonable response.

After the first interview, I ask if the opportunity is good enough to consider a lateral move. I do not care what the answer is, yes or no. When I do this, interest in the opportunity goes up, and the compensation demands come down. Inversely, as compensation demands increase, interest in the opportunity decreases. It is a variable. If somebody is asking for more and more money as the process goes on, it is an indicator for you to go deeper into that process to uncover what is holding them back or see if they are just kicking tires.

Compensation is not the only negotiating point to

consider when talking to candidates. Many organizations have a reasonably static vacation policy. I have seen people negotiate more paid vacation time if they already have a lot of vacation time at their current organization. The benefits package is usually pretty standard. Companies can compensate for that by offering a sign-on bonus to make up for superior benefits or wave the usual waiting period for medical benefits. Some organizations are also using open to negotiating remote work or flexible hours.

## DEALING WITH COUNTEROFFERS

One of the biggest frustrations for both the client and the recruiter is going through this entire process and then the candidate receives a counteroffer. What is your best strategy to prevent this from happening?

The risk of a counteroffer – or a turndown for that matter – is why you must go through the process of determining the candidate's wants and needs at the onset of the process. It is why you check in with the candidate throughout the interview and offer negotiation processes. The candidate's potential to receive a counteroffer is something you want to start tackling on the first call, especially with a passive candidate.

Understand all of the minor imperfections at the candidate's current organization and then explore those imperfections at every step in the interview process. When you help a candidate notice issues they have in their current position, they become more aware of them. These annoyances multiply during an interview process. That is just how the brain works. Throughout the interview process, I want to hear the candidate talk about their attraction to the company, what they are going to, and what they are leaving.

One of the best ways to prevent a counteroffer is asking,

at the beginning of the process, "What could your company do to keep you?"

You want to *dig* here.

- What if they promoted you?

- What if you receive a 10 percent raise from my client and they match it?

- What if they promise to "fix" the things you are talking about with me?

If they waver and say they would consider staying, I propose that they should have a conversation with their boss right away. They should ask for some time with him or her and review what is bothering them. Ask their boss, "What's your vision for me at this organization twelve to twenty-four months from now?"

I will then share with the candidate the two most likely ways that conversation will go. Their manager will tell them to leave them alone and go back to work by saying, "That is something I do not want to deal with now." Or their manager will say, "I had no idea you wanted to have this conversation. Let us set a time for lunch."

Based on the response, the company is revealing its genuine interest in the candidate. If the current manager is earnest about having that conversation, the candidate and manager will have an honest conversation about career growth. If the manager ignores the candidate and then makes a counteroffer, you know it is not a sincere counteroffer.

I admit, I lost candidates in this process when they had a conversation about career growth. The loss was not to a counteroffer. They disengaged after the first or second interview, saying they fixed their problem at work. I never considered it a total loss. Even though I did not place that candidate with my client, I helped another human being *and* I saved myself and my client from a successful counteroffer.

When you tell a candidate to have that conversation, even if they do not, it is tough for them to accept a counteroffer at the time of the offer. My goal throughout the entire process is to help the candidate clarify why they are leaving and what they are going to and then constantly reminding them of those two things as I go through the process.

The Definition of Acceptance is the process of leading a candidate to clarify what they want and need. For my recruiters and me, we took every candidate through this strenuous Definition of Acceptance process. The outcome with each candidate was an understanding that when they say "yes" to the offer, even verbally, they are saying, "No, I will not make a counteroffer. No, I will not consider competing offers."

Once you get to the final offer stage, you have gone through the process of flushing all that out. Again, you are not abruptly going through this at the end of the interview process. If the interview process took a month, these are questions you ask the candidate to go back to and investigate throughout the month-long process. You do not want them to take an opportunity they do not want, and you want them to accept a job that they fully intend on showing up for.

## FINAL THOUGHTS

Flawless Execution is the presentation of a strong enough portfolio of candidates to choose from. Your client has numerous candidates to invite to interview and extend an offer. If the client's first choice turns down the offer or takes a counteroffer, there is a backup candidate. While every niche is different, Flawless Execution will always lead to you becoming a trusted advisor. Your clients will know that they can rely on two or three outstanding candidates every time they give you a search, which increases the likelihood of you getting exclusives, retainers, higher fees, and repeat business.

# FLAWLESS EXECUTION CASE STUDY

## KATHY NUNNALLY ANEMOGIANNIS – REGIONS EXECUTIVE RECRUITING

Kathy Nunnally Anemogiannis is the founder of Regions Executive Recruiting, based in Atlanta, Georgia. Regions Executive Recruiting specializes in placing executives in the manufacturing and wholesale distribution, commercial real estate, and construction industries.

## HOW DO YOU FIND AND DEVELOP GREAT PASSIVE CANDIDATES?

Naturally, start with research. At this point, I have been in business for more than ten years, so I have a database of candidates. But always – in addition to checking the database – do the research. I have a researcher based in Bangladesh who does that for me. Finding passive candidates is the same process as marketing to find clients.

One of the biggest things I have gotten out of working with The RecruiterU is coming at things from the perspective of their needs, so leading, not coming at it from, "My client needs a new BPS supply chain." It is when they pick up the phone, and I chat with them. It is using some variation of that line that Mike learned from Peter Lefkowitz: "I am not sure where you are with your career, what your ambitions are, but we are representing an opportunity on behalf of a client. I would love to hear where you are career-wise," and just coming at it from their needs. It is that simple.

## ONCE YOU GO THROUGH THAT PROCESS AND THE CANDIDATE RECEIVES A JOB OFFER, HOW DO YOU NEGOTIATE THAT OFFER WITH THE CANDIDATE TO ENSURE THEY ARE NOT TAKING A COUNTEROFFER?

Preventing a counteroffer does not start with the candidate getting the offer. I am constantly working; I call it enrollment. I am enrolling that candidate in this opportunity as we move through the different wickets and the different gateways in the process. I am constantly checking in with them, taking their pulse. I hear if there are any concerns. I am going to know about those along the way.

I ask the candidate if they hear anything incongruous

from talking with one person and then the next during the interview process. It is constantly taking the pulse, communicating, talking with them, and then drawing them back to what I originally heard that they shared with me. I'm going back to what was intriguing about the opportunity, what it was going to offer them. I'm taking them back to what the value was going to be in this position, what the attraction was going to be about this position. When the offer comes, I am not working that hard to make sure they take it. They want it.

We address if they anticipate receiving a counteroffer. So, we are talking about that early on. I cannot think – honestly – of anyone who took a counteroffer in the past five years. I cannot.

## IS THERE ANYTHING ELSE YOU WOULD SHARE ON JUST FINDING CANDIDATES?

Communication is key. The biggest compliment I hear from candidates is that they acknowledge me as "the best recruiter I have ever worked with," or they say, "You are one of the best recruiters I've ever worked with." And it is that communication. Even if the client is not advancing – maybe we have lost a little momentum for a couple of days because of, I don't know, whatever reason – I am going back to those candidates and saying, "Hey, my update is I have no update," and they appreciate it.

Just the fact that I am checking in and letting them know we still have not forgotten about them – they are still out there, so those regular communications are really key. They acknowledge me for that. It creates good clients. Those candidates become my client down the road.

I have a situation right now: a VP of HR that I had placed a year ago – she always tells her employer, "If it weren't for

Kathy, I wouldn't be here," because the process really slowed, and so I had to keep her engaged. I would send funny cards in the mail like, "I know it has been six weeks since we first talked, but I set your expectations that this would be a pretty long process." It is all about engagement. Now, I am getting business from her because she is like, "Yeah, I want anyone we talk with to have a similar experience to what I had because it really gave me a great feeling for this company. If they were investing in someone like you to attract me, I want to do that for any strategic hiring needs that we have."

That is the heart of Flawless Execution for me.

# PART 3: CREATING A SELF-DRIVING BUSINESS

GOING FROM FOUNDER DEPENDENT TO TEAM RUN!

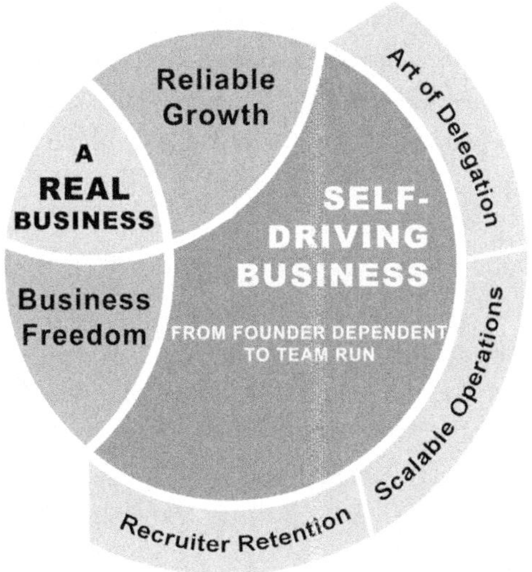

Most recruiting firms are solo operations. While I do not have exact data, in my experience, this is true with around 50 to 65 percent of the firms on our marketing list.

There are many valid reasons why you may want to stay a solo operator. On the other hand, some recruiters remain solo practitioners because of a limiting belief on what scaling a firm could look like. In my training seminars, I ask the room why those that are solo chose to stay solo. The most common response is "freedom" and "flexibility."

If you *truly* desire freedom and flexibility, the worst business model is a solo operation! Why? You are *never* free. You are not free on vacation or your days off. You need to check emails, voicemails, texts, chats, et cetera, on deals in progress. You need to return emails and calls from everyone. You are constantly tied to your business.

Additionally, while you are relaxing, new business and candidate development *stops*. The business is entirely dependent on you, the owner, to drive all production. While this does provide some flexibility, it provides almost no freedom.

If freedom and flexibility are the goals of being self-employed, I have found no better way than building a recruiting firm that can run without you there. I ran both. I was solo, and I also built a multi-million-dollar firm. I had far more flexibility and freedom (never mind cashflow) in my scaled recruiting firm.

If that is true (and it is), then why don't more firms scale their operations? Most recruiters were taught the wrong way to build a firm. The model to scale a recruiting firm in the twenty-first century still mostly resembles the structure designed in the 1960s:

1. Hire straight commission or draw versus commission salespeople who have never worked in recruitment before

2. Teach them the entire business in two to three weeks (while running your desk)

3. Provide little to no daily accountability

4. Prayer (a *lot* of prayer)

My fears of people messing things up (they do early on, but you fix that) were not realized. One of my first big delegations was getting people to recruit on my open searches. The thought of doing this paralyzed me. I was afraid my recruiter would not serve my clients at the level I served them. Not only did this *not* happen, but many of the recruiters (who had *no* recruiting experience when I hired them) became better sourcers of talent than I was in a short time. The key to this was having a system to teach them how to recruit the right way.

Do you see the theme yet? Your ability to grow your business is dependent on the systems first and the team second. With the right systems in place, you can put a new person into that system and continue to grow your firm.

# 10

# ART OF DELEGATION

Delegation is an area where most of the clients we work with struggle the most. Delegation is not yet cultural in the recruiting industry. How to effectively delegate aspects of your recruiting practice, as a solo recruiters and a firm owner alike, is not discussed at conferences or in traditional training programs. Instead, the topics focus on getting clients, taking job orders, finding and recruiting candidates, hiring recruiters, and managing your team. There is rarely a conversation around the art of delegating. But delegating is, indeed, an art.

## CREATING A CULTURE OF DELEGATION IN RECRUITING

***Why is a culture of delegation missing in recruiting?***

The most common barrier to creating a culture of delegation in recruiting is the pervasive attitude held by recruiters. That attitude – which is not entirely incorrect but does hold them back in scaling their desk or firm – is, "I do it better than anybody else here." That "it" is usually recruiting. The firm owner believes they are only person who can identify great talent because nobody understands their niche as well as they do.

I possessed that same attitude and held the same beliefs for the first decade of my career. I was reluctant to delegate anything in my business. I was terrified anyone I gave the assignment to would "mess it up" and negatively affect my reputation.

It is comical to think of this now, but I had a full-time admin and didn't delegate ordering office supplies because I thought I could get pads of paper for $1 cheaper. For the longest time, it never occurred to me how much time I wasted going through the Staples catalog to find $100 worth of office supplies for $10 of savings.

The attitude of "I am the only one who can do it" that many solo recruiters and firm owners hang onto is holding them back. It is a significant blind spot that we see in many of the clients in our coaching programs. Many recruiting firm owners and recruiters are in a default control mode mainly because they put together deals.

This default of control is a result of how many recruiting firms develop. No one goes to school to get a degree in recruiting. Recruiting firms are built by people with an entrepreneurial drive, even if they do not consider themselves entrepreneurs. We work with many clients who built their firms from the ground up without the help or guidance of a franchise organization or any formal training. Early in their career, doing the research and administrative work was a means of learning the profession and managing expenses. As their businesses grew, they became so accustomed to doing it all that delegating felt scary and hard.

There is also a perception that it is significantly harder to delegate than just to do it yourself. Because you have been performing these functions for so long, you minimize the tasks. You might think, "I can do it myself. It is just looking at profiles on LinkedIn or sending out an invoice. I will just do it myself so I don't have to pay someone to do the research or administrative work."

## COMPUTING THE REAL COST OF DOING IT ALL YOURSELF

Recruiters with this attitude or belief fail to compute the total value of their time and money that is lost. For example, if a solo operator or a recruiter in a firm bills $300,000 a year at forty hours per week, their bill rate is about $150 an hour. For comparison, if that person worked in a law or accounting firm, they would be billing the same rate.

As a recruiter with a $300,000 desk, your conservative hourly rate is $150. At that rate, many recruiters do not delegate a task like research, which is a $10- to $15-an-hour role. The reason? "I'm the *best* researcher/ profiler." Fun fact: you're *not!* When you outsource research to the right company, they do it quicker and better than you at less than 10 percent of what it costs you to do it!

This calculation is where the belief of doing it yourself saves money does not stand the test of reason. Every hour you do your own research costs them $140. At the recruiting firm level, there is a $140 per billing hour per recruiting desk loss to save $10 or $15 an hour in research.

To liberate yourself or your team to do what you truly do best (e.g., conversations with a hiring manager and candidate, then managing that process): maximize. Doing research or administrative work is a vital part of the business, but that can be accomplished by someone whose sole purpose is to perform those tasks.

## WHAT TO DELEGATE IN YOUR RECRUITING PRACTICE

What are some of the most important areas of the business to delegate?

### *Research*

Delegating research is the first area to delegate in your practice. Within the first month of working with a recruiting firm owner or a solo operator, we advise them to hire a researcher if they have not already done so. A researcher is someone who will find names, phone numbers, and email addresses for people in your target market. The researcher can gather information for both the prospect side for your marketing list and the recruiting side for your open searches.

If research is the first most crucial area to delegate, why do so many resist doing so? The answer, "I can look at a LinkedIn profile and see somebody that is perfect" is not untrue. However, a researcher will have to spend ten times as much time as you to break even. Recall that for every hour you spend doing your own research, you are losing $140 in revenue. The researcher will stumble upon the same candidates as you, and many researchers have licenses to LinkedIn Recruiter and other tools. That access allows you to redirect funds from purchasing subscriptions for yourself or your team.

Research is the number one thing I recommend delegating.

### *Administrative Support*

If you are a firm owner or even a solo operator, administrative support is the next area of the business I recommend delegating after research. If you are a recruiting firm owner – especially if you have a team of recruiters and do not have at least a part-time administrative assistant – you are losing a minimum of $100,000 to $200,000 a year by not delegating this.

An administrative assistant can handle the numerous distracting tasks that are part of the search process, which will allow you and your team to stay focused. That includes entering data, tracking, entering job orders, ensuring candidates are entered correctly, quickly importing resumes, ensuring proper tagging in your database. An administrative assistant can do all of this.

Honestly, if you do not have administrative support, you are either not doing these tasks or doing them inconsistently, which means you are losing access to the data. Lost data results in a lost time and revenue. If your recruiters perform these tasks, it keeps them from doing what they do best: talking with clients and prospects. When you and your team are not doing what you do best, you are losing revenue.

## HOW DELEGATION SAVES TIMES AND INCREASES REVENUE

Outsourcing your research and administrative support saves money and allows you to grow your revenue. But how do these resources free up your time specifically? What are some of the other benefits gained, productivity-wise, from delegating?

When you delegate something, it might take you longer than the initial period of one to two weeks. During this initiation phase, you might still be doing a little bit of the work yourself as you train the researcher or administrative assistant. During this time, it is unproductive to think it just would be easier if you continued to do it yourself. At the moment, yes, it is, but it is important to see beyond that moment. By working with a researcher or adding administrative support, you regain the several hours back each day.

For example, imagine that you start each day with a great list of people to contact. Instead of showing up to your desk and not having the correct list to call or email, if you set up the right cadence with a researcher, they can easily find two to five hundred names for you to contact a week. Of course, you will never talk to five hundred people in a week, but now you have a qualified list.

When you hire a researcher, you must treat them as a member of your team. Set clear expectations on not only the data but also presentation of the data. You cannot assume that the researcher will validate phone numbers and email addresses if you do not explicitly ask them to do so. After each submission, give the researcher constructive feedback so they can continuously refine their output. In that first few weeks, the list from a researcher will not be perfect – far from it!

The right researcher will give you increasingly better lists as they learn more about your requirements and niche. Remember, they are experts at research, *not* in your niche! Even if it takes a few weeks or a month of working closely with your researcher during this training period, think about the amount of time you would have had to spend on LinkedIn or ZoomInfo to create a list.

Indeed, I know a lot of people who like doing their own research. Many times, doing their own research is a means of productive procrastination. By doing research, they can justify to themselves that they are working, and this also allows them to avoid making cold recruiting or marketing calls. The significant benefit is that when you go through the process of delegating, you have no excuse not to focus on the things that will generate revenue.

When you begin focusing solely on those revenue-generating activities, everything else falls into place. Armed with a great list of people to contact daily and administrative support to keep your database organized, you can focus on your marketing, recruiting, and deal-making conversations. You can focus on consistently following up with prospects and candidates. Through all this focused activity, you will gain more searches, find better talent for your clients, and close more deals.

## WHERE TO FIND RESEARCH AND ADMINISTRATIVE SUPPORT

The first hurdle to overcome is moving beyond believing that no one can do things better than you. The next hurdle is finding highly qualified research and administrative support professionals, which is where some people get stuck. They are unsure of where to find support, so they stay stuck.

When we realized that not knowing where to find support held some of our clients back from delegating, we created a resource page of trusted partners, vetted by The RecruiterU and our clients.

Regardless of if your work with a vetted partner or find someone on your own, remember that nobody is perfect. For example, if you work with a research company, that company will dedicate a trained researcher to you. However, just because they have training in the basics of research, you will also need to train and work with them closely on your business needs.

Again, it is always a little bit bumpy in the beginning. For example, you may give the researcher a project to find fifty widget engineers that work within a thirty-mile radius of San Jose. Your researcher will find good ones and not-so-good ones. As you work with that researcher, refine the process continuously. This feedback will allow you to see where you were not clear when setting expectations. Coach them on why some of the names were good, why some were just okay, and why some were not good at all. Tell them they did well and correct what they did not do well.

Some clients have had great experiences working with dedicated research providers. Other clients prefer to use a freelancer marketplace like Upwork or Fiverr. On these sites, you post the job. For example, you can develop a list of 500 candidates who are software engineers within a fifty-mile radius of San Jose with specific criteria. Freelancers will then submit their interest in working with you and bid on the job. You will have to work with five to ten freelancers to find the one that works best with you.

A best practice during this vetting process is to give each freelancer a small project. This project is an investment of $30 to $50 each. The purpose of giving them all the same project is to evaluate ability, turnaround times, and the quality of the information provided.

A significant pitfall many people make is hiring just one freelancer at a time. If you are hiring someone on a freelancer marketplace like Upwork or Fiverr, do not hire one; hire several. By hiring several and giving them an identical assignment, you can vet them through an apples-to-apples comparison.

If you hire a research company, you can hire just one. However, regardless of where you hire your research or administrative support, make sure you have a precise process and concrete outcomes that you want, especially from the researcher.

One of the most important things to realize is that your research and administrative support does not need to be in-house. You do not need to hire another employee for your firm. The beauty of delegating this type of support through a provider or freelancer is that you can leverage people who could be anywhere in the world to do work for you.

With some of the research companies, you may have to make a small commitment. The commitment and investment are nominal. If you use a freelance marketplace like Upwork or Fiverr, you can hire on a per-project basis. The nice thing with Upwork – and potentially a research company – is that it is like a thermostat. You can turn it up and down depending on the activity on your desk. Providing that the freelancer you found is available, you can give them more work, and they will charge you per project or hour. During slower periods, you can pull back.

The benefit of this flexibility is you can still work with the same researcher on a project-by-project basis but not incur the fixed overhead costs of payroll taxes, benefits, and all those other things associated with having somebody full time. With a project-based person, the research is contingent upon the work that comes in.

## THE DELEGATION PROCESS

As mentioned earlier, delegating may feel a little challenging in the beginning because you are teaching someone how to do something. What are some essential things to know within the delegation process?

Most entrepreneurs – never mind recruiting firm owners – suffer the problem of drive-by delegations. Full transparency: I am guilty of committing an occasional drive-by delegation. Drive-by delegation is when you give the person those couple of quick items or ideas that come to your mind. You say something like, "Hey, take care of this for me." In doing so, you give them only pieces or aspects of the projects, but not the entire scope expecting the person to whom you delegated to figure out what is missing based on their interpretation of the information provided.

In drive-by delegation, you essentially expect the person you are delegating to read your mind. You expect them to know where you are in the process or what steps to complete the task or project. They have to make their best guess on what success looks like for them. As the person who engages in drive-by delegation, you become frustrated when the team member asks multiple questions or does not produce the anticipated results quickly.

*"Expectations are resentments waiting to happen."*

— ANNE LAMOTT

The way to avoid that is to sit down with a piece of paper and map out what you want to delegate. For delegation to succeed, establish specific criteria, including the desired outcome.

I decide that I wanted to delegate database entry; the desired outcome was to have all data in our company entered. We had many recruiters who kept paper resumes and notes in a folder. We had a CRM, and I wanted information in the system, but I did not want the recruiters entering it.

This was my process: When the recruiter completed a search, the administrative assistant took the search folder from the recruiter and entered the critical data points. They did not enter everything, only the main criteria on each candidate from their resume. These criteria included an updated resume for each candidate, proper labeling/ coding of the candidate and recruiter, and other vital details. The process and criteria were outlined so anyone in the administrative assistant role could pick up that task and understand what needed to be entered.

Our recruiters and I were possessive of our paper folders. The administrative assistant took folders from the recruiters when the search was over to enter the information. Then, once the data entry was complete, they handed the folder back to them to discard the paper, file the paper, or do whatever they wanted to do. The benefit of this process, especially for those that own a firm, is that so much information is sitting on Post-It notes and random pages of a legal pad. If another recruiter has a similar search assignment, they cannot access that data because it is sitting on paper somewhere.

Delegating data entry is just one example of how to delegate successfully. The basic steps to successful delegation are:

1. Clearly defining what success looks like in delegation for this specific project or task.

2. Clearly outlining the steps or criteria for the project or task.

3. Reviewing the steps or criteria to ensure you did not miss anything important to a successful outcome. We often miss important information, especially if we have been performing this task ourselves because we do things automatically. (The litmus test is when you read the success criteria and the steps, you would be happy with that outcome done that way)

The first time you delegate something, it is best to meet with the person you are delegating to give and receive feedback on the process. Do not wait until they are days/ weeks deep or nearing completion of the project. Be proactive as they begin work. Ask if there are any areas of confusion. Ask them to restate, step by step, what you just delegated to them to gauge their understanding.

After a short time, also gauge if they received resistance from anyone on the team. By checking in at the onset instead of waiting, you can answer questions and provide course correction immediately. This avoid friction between you and your team member when expectations are not met.

Once you go through this delegation once with somebody, you may need to invest 10 or 15 percent or the same amount of time the next time. However, each time you go through this process, that investment decreases until the process runs independently. That decreasing investment is why delegation is a critical component for going from founder-dependent to team-run. If you insist on doing everything yourself, you are never going to have a real business. You will have a nice job or practice but not a real business.

## FINAL THOUGHTS

Numerous clients, especially those with small teams, have fought with us regarding delegation. However, once they finally decide to give delegation a try, they say,

- "You know what, thanks for staying on me so I finally outsourced research or hired an admin."

- "I cannot believe how much more money I am making."

- "I cannot believe how much more time I have."

- "I cannot believe how much less stress I have because of letting it go!"

- "I can't believe how much better the person is at it than I."

- "I used to think I was the only one who could do it, but I was proven wrong."

The critical area for me when I ultimately started delegating was recruiting on my searches. My desk was mostly doing retained work. I was incredibly insecure about hiring somebody to do the search. When hiring, I clearly defined my search process and completely outlined what a completed search process looks like.

I walked my new recruiters through what a successful outcome looked like, and then I coached the person through it. With our business now, I had similar insecurity about delegating coaching. I believed that people hired me to be their coach. The reality was, no, they hired me to get a *result* in their company they were struggling to get on their own. We get that result through a defined coaching process that yields that result. Ultimately, our clients were investing in a better version of themselves and their business, not me as an individual.

When thinking about your business, especially in terms of delegation, it is important to remember that everything is process driven. Processes build systems. Systems and processes are replicable.

Take a hard look at everything that you are doing. What tasks do you think only you can do well? Ask yourself if performing that task is the best use of your time. Most likely, it is not. There is a process for delegating to someone who, with the proper guidance, can successfully do it for you – probably even better than you.

# ART OF DELEGATION CASE STUDY

## MARK REISNER – MERWIN GROUP

Mark Reisner is the managing director of the Merwin Group, located in Pennsylvania, specializing in recruitment for the electric generation, transmission, and generation industry. Mark founded his consulting and recruitment practice in 2004 as an outshoot of his career path and passion for building businesses within businesses. After six million air miles and twelve corporate relocations, he decided to finally put down roots and join a franchise organization, which helped him get started. Since then, he admits to having some great wins and some great losses but growing from these experiences. The Art of Delegation allowed Mark to work smarter, not harder.

## WHAT FUNCTIONS DID YOU OUTSOURCE IN YOUR RECRUITING PRACTICE?

Literally everything. Years ago, I saw that you could harness the power of technology to make a positive difference in people's lives with these technological advantages. In recruiting especially, I saw the benefits for people who were tired of going to the office – "tired of herding cats" is the way I always described it – and having teams in bullpens. There is nothing wrong with that model, but it was not my cup of tea.

It was painful to make that switch, so the first step had to be having a system. I happen to use PCRecruiter (an applicant tracking system), but it does not matter as long as you make sure that you have a very compact yet versatile system to communicate. Before the Zooms of the world, I invested a great deal in very expensive video conferencing, but that has gone by the wayside because video conferencing is so powerful now.

So, I have outsourced first research. I have been working on effectively outsourcing research for seventeen years. I tried and kissed many, many frogs over the years and constantly had to circle back to the fact that they had people that would take the time and quality over volume and validation over anything else to confirm their information.

I tried a number of different approaches for actually outsourcing recruiting. That became a little bit more difficult, but what has dramatically improved is ease and speed in video conferencing. You have to have that interpersonal relationship. You have to be able to see into their eyes, and you have to see their desktop. If you don't have that ability, you are limited in outsourcing recruiters because recruiters are great at picking up the phone and selling and what have you. Still, they are not in the discipline world of recorded results, recorded metrics, and recording activity. Where is their positive? Where is their negative?

Part of seeing the power of PCRecruiter has been astronomical, and being able to do that – you still have to be able to have the eyes on. I failed miserably in hiring recruiters. I got myself in a big jam two years ago because I received what many people would consider the most incredible search assignment. I had thirty positions – all exactly the same, more blue-collar – but would still require all of the needs, and I received the engagement fee of 40 percent for all of those, and I had partners lined up to help me.

I had other offices. I had the world's largest recruiting firm with manpower lined up, and every one of them failed miserably. I was in big trouble because I had made these commitments, and I did not have the resources behind me at the time that could deliver. I had people, but they just did not have the mindset to deliver what we needed or the research to find them.

So, we peeled back the onion quickly.

I tried a number of firms, primarily in the Philippines because the big advantage there is language. They are culturally more attuned to recruiting than other places in the world. I hired people, and they were provided office space. It was a managing challenge. I finally came upon another organization that was geared up to develop recruiters, develop salespeople.

There are two functions in recruiting. One is actually

securing a search assignment or a job order, which is the marketing expertise; and then the expertise to contact people and convince them. Through my years of study with that other franchise organization, we found by far and away the most successful organizations were people that separated and were not full cycle recruiters doing everything. So, the long and short of it, I found this resource, it has turned out to be a phenomenal partnership.

Success is really developing that partnership, which is true if you have an office and people around you. The best recruiters, the best people, are your partners. I found an ability to do a partnership by having daily video conferences and feedback. If there has ever been a term that our industry has misused, it is feedback. We always want it from our clients, but we do not give it to others. Be diligent in giving feedback. Tell people why something is bad, not right, or off-kilter – whatever you want to call it – and show them by giving them examples. Feedback is not just patting them on the back and saying, "You did great on this or that." Give people constant feedback so they can they become better.

Now, I will share with you a little insight. Yesterday, the hiring manager in Georgia texted my leader of the division and said, "I need sixteen individuals." She emailed our head recruiter in the Philippines, and within twenty minutes, she had a text message out to 850-something candidate prospects within a 100-mile radius of where we needed them. She and the team over there are on the phone, and we have profiles coming in. At 9:30 this morning, the head of the division was able to get six candidates to the hiring manager.

And that all happens because it is all outsourced.

You build that partnership – and that is the word that I used before. The partnership is so vitally important so that they become an integral partner of what you are doing. You let them know what the client is doing.

## IN YOUR OPINION, THE CRITICAL FACTOR FOR SUCCESS WHEN OUTSOURCING IS CREATING A PARTNERSHIP WITH COMMUNICATION AND FEEDBACK?

Absolutely correct. I am happy because someone contacted me who heard me speak at one of your sessions that was mindset related to the excellence of recruiting, and it was a fabulous session. She hemmed and hawed, and she contacted me about ten days afterward. She decided that she wanted to see if she could join up with me, and we are into that breaking-in process. I am learning the mindset of patience and tolerance.

Another part of outsourcing is that when you dig down, you have to be patient and tolerant. You need not overwhelm them with information but do it in little bite-sized chunks and do it daily. So, we have a video conference twice a day for ten minutes. She said she was exhausted last night, but she was on the phone for the first time. The first time, I did not let her get on the phone for a week and gave her all the specific roll up, fifteen calls, two job orders, and one referral.

## HOW DID OUTSOURCING CHANGE NOT ONLY YOUR BUSINESS BUT YOUR LIFE?

I can do my job and manage my team from anywhere. I was on a cruise on my way to St. Lucia. I got a text at 9:00 a.m., forwarded to my phone, on the ship, out at sea in the Caribbean, and by 11:00 a.m., we had three candidates interviewed, offers sent that afternoon, and that was Thursday. They started the following Monday while I was still on the cruise.

The freedom – technology means a whole heck of a lot, and I use a phone system that can get me anywhere in the world. I am terrible about making calls. I hate it. It is the bane of every recruiter – I should not say every recruiter, but the vast majority of us.

I am in energy, and there is a huge, huge need for batteries – astronomical. Some of these car company's valuation is just crazy. Last Monday, I sent my researcher to find ten mid-start startup companies, so I just gave them that criteria. We ended up with eight of them. I sent an email to forty-five names at eight companies yesterday at 11:00 a.m.

I made three calls to the twelve or thirteen or fourteen that opened the email and got a callback from the chief technology officer. His first question was, "How did you get the CEO's telephone number? How did you do it? He does not give that to anyone. You have got to promise me how to do it." The long and the short of it, we had a great conversation. He said, "Clearly, you know what you are doing in your industry," blah, blah, blah.

I will not go into all of the details, but that conversation resulted from outsourcing researching. My researcher set everything up in my contact management system. They set up the roll-up call list. I whipped together a The RecruiterU MPC email for my MPC candidate on Sunday afternoon. Now, I have a search assignment for two that will turn into engaged. It does not always work that way, but I emphasize that you have still got to make the calls no matter what. But sometimes, you can find people who will make the calls for you. That is the diamond in the rough in outsourcing.

# 11

# SCALABLE OPERATIONS

Scalable Operations: what most recruiting firms do not have because they were never taught the right way to scale their firm. I started my recruiting firm in a franchise system. In hindsight, I was never taught the right way to scale my recruiting business. While the franchise I was in provided a strong foundation, they supported the traditional model of hiring full desk recruiters to scale a business. This antiquated traditional model is holding recruiting firm owners back from successfully scaling their business. The traditional way you were taught to hire and scale our recruiting firms is dead.

## WHY THE TRADITIONAL MODEL OF HIRING IS DEAD

The way you were taught to hire recruiters is what keeps you playing small. Less than 10 percent of recruiting firms ever achieve over seven figures in revenue, but the same is not true for legal firms, accounting firms, consulting companies, and other professional service firms. The reason is because of how you grow our team.

You were taught to teach new recruiters everything: how to market, how to recruit, how to prep, how to close, how to negotiate deals, the vernacular of the niche they are in, et cetera. Not only do you teach them all of this, but you are also expecting them to learn it all in less than a month.

The traditional model of hiring is overwhelming. It is what I went through when I first started to scale my firm, and it almost put me out of business. In this model, seven to ten recruiters need to be hired to keep one. These metrics are demotivating as well as expensive. The thought that went through my mind when hiring using the traditional model was, "Goodness, even if I bring on two people, they are probably not going to make it. All of that work to recruit, interview, and train, and maybe one will survive." You developed similar belief systems around failure, and you have the evidence, based on the system you were taught, that it would fail. It becomes a vicious cycle.

The other reason the traditional hiring model is dead is pay. The traditional model of hiring is based on straight commission or incredibly low draws versus commission. When people are looking for a new career, they seek a position that has the appearance of a real job – more importantly, a possible new career. They want to excitedly say to their partner, family, and friends that they are joining a new organization that is paying them this salary with these benefits and the potential to make even more as they grow in their role. The best talent wants a "real job" that has a salary and benefits.

The straight commission or 50 percent compensation plan is a relic. This compensation structure was engineered when we had index cards for our candidate and clients databases. These index cards and telephone lines were the primary overhead on a desk. The compensation structure was also designed when you could offer insurance benefits for a family that cost only about $250 a month with a $200 deductible. Insurance premiums have skyrocketed over the past decade. Now, that same family plan might be $2,500 or $3,000 a month.

There is a complete disconnect when you look at how the recruiting firm industry scales versus how other professional service firms scale. There is only one role in a recruiting firm. This role is either called an account executive or a search consultant. You start and end your tenure with the firm in that role; there is no evolution beyond it. So, that career path model is not scalable from the standpoint of building a firm that is not only seven figures but multi-seven figures.

### *Roles of Recruiters*

When I studied how other professional services firms scaled, I rarely found a career path where someone began and ended in the same role. Instead, the usual progression was starting in a role that focused on one aspect of the business. Then, in time, that person advanced in a role that built upon the previous one or focused on a different aspect of the business.

For a solo recruiter, the first step to scale is to outsource your research. As mentioned in Chapter 7, you should not be going through LinkedIn profiles – if you do, you should only be spending a maximum of a few hours a week doing so. The first step to scaling the business is outsourcing research. It is the path of least resistance. You do not have to hire someone; you can hire a research firm or a freelancer.

Once you get into a scaling mode where you want to build a team, start hiring entry-level recruiters, which I call is search associated. This job title is in alignment with other professional service firms that hire associates.

A search associate is someone whose sole function is finding and identifying talent on your existing open searches. A search associate develops their phone and conversation skills through recruiting calls. They learn what questions to ask to dig deep into a potential candidate's qualifications, motivations, and availability to make a career move. A search associate remains in this role until they master it. Mastery is determined through accountability structures and achieved when they are consistent with their metrics from Recruiter GPS.

Once a search associate masters their role, you can transition them into a new role of account executive. As an account executive, they now take all the skills that they developed as a search associate and build upon them by teaching them how to market.

At this stage, when you teach a new account executive marketing, they already know the vernacular of the industry. They already know what an excellent search assignment looks like because they have been working on your search assignments. They already know what the flow of a deal looks like because you have involved them in that process. Now, you just layer upon these skills by teaching the small chunk of marketing. Marketing is not an easy skill to master, but by layering on top of their skills in recruiting, you are setting them up for success. It is at this stage that you have them develop their own assignments.

Over time, the account executive will get to a point where they are consistent with both their marketing and recruiting, and they are not working on your material anymore. At this point, they are working on their own and become the account executive that you wanted to (or were taught to) hire maybe a year before.

By taking the time to teach each part of the process and allowing them to master each part before moving onto the next, that recruiter is much more successful and much more profitable. More important, your turnover rate is 3.5 times less when you bring them on first as a search associate and then promoting them to an account executive versus hiring them to do all the aspects of the business from day one.

When an account executive becomes really good in their role and successfully developing new business, you want to leverage that business development skill set. At this point, you can further scale your team by promoting them to the role of practice leader.

As a practice leader you can hire search associates to do some, but not all of the recruiting for them. for example, you have an account executive doing $20,000 per month or a $250,000 run rate. by hiring a search associate for them you can take that desk/ practice to $400,000 to $500,000 per year by having them work on openings the account executive develops but does not have time to work.

Practice leaders do not stop recruiting. If the practice leader sets up three first-time interviews a week, you can layer in a search associate to arrange an additional two first-time interviews each week. Between the practice leader and search associate, the team is doubling production by leveraging the business development acumen of the practice leader.

Now, instead of hiring someone, teaching them the entire process, and expecting them to master it all at once, you are creating a career path that emphasizes proficiency and mastery at each level. This scaffolded approach to career development builds confidence and motivation while decreasing turnover.

When I used this approach to scale my firm, I never had a big biller leave my firm. Recruiters in my firm that we defined as a pacesetter, who were able to earn the President's Club trip, never left our firm because there was always another step in their career development and another challenge for them to conquer. It is important to note that not only did I retain my team member, but none of them were paid using the archaic 50 percent commission structure. My recruiters were paid using a compensation structure that included a base salary plus commission and benefits.

This type of career path leads to higher retention. In the traditional hiring model, you build somebody to where they are performing well, billing between $300,000 or $400,000 a year. After four or five years, many want to go off independently. Many times, this desire had nothing to do with the owner. In my many conversations with recruiters, they have nothing but respect for the person that hired them. But they do the math. They see that they are billing $400,000, and of that revenue, the owner gets $200,000, and they get $200,000. The recruiter questions what they get for their $200,000 from the owner. They believe the owner/ manager is no longer providing value or enough value to justify "turning over" half of their billings.

I always ask myself, "What do I have to do to earn the amount that I keep as the business owner?"

The answer to this question is how you define the value you are giving back to your recruiters. That answer will transition into retention and how you are scaffolding the career in your firm. You bring value to your recruiters by always setting up the next challenge for them. Hold a vision for them and get them further in their careers than they could do alone.

## ELEMENTS OF A MODERN COMPENSATION PLAN

Most recruiting firms have a compensation plan that looks like the one I hate. When we take on a new coaching client, I often find some remnant of the old-fashioned 50 percent agreement or a lot of straight-commission type language.

Many still try to hire straight commission or with a small draw versus commission. I always ask people who are hesitant to move to a salary from a draw that if somebody quits after three months and you paid them a $2,000 a month draw, how much of that money do you get back? The answer is none of it. Therefore, if you paid them a $2,000 a month salary, in effect, you have the same result. (Let me be clear, I am not recommending a salary of $2,000 a month; I am using this figure for argument's sake.)

Regardless of the amount of salary paid per month, you get the same result. When that person goes home to their parents, significant other, or friends and talks about a job with a base salary, even if it is a lower base salary, it is still a base-salary job. It is a real job versus one that sounds like straight commission. It is a connotation that is unnecessary.

Additionally, I do not advise that you pay the base salary plus the 25 percent starting or 20 percent starting commission rates. I advise that you pay a base salary of $3,000 a month. On top of that base salary, only pay 10 percent on the first $10,000 brought in every month. Then, pay 30 to 35 percent over the first $10,000 in a month. In the end, you will pay out less per $100,000 than you would on the old compensation plans with no more risk.

An excellent plan that retains recruiters and allows you to scale has a salary element, a benefits element, and a commission element that pays a higher percentage on higher incomes but pays only 5 percent or 10 percent on the first $100,000 cash-in per year.

## WHEN TO SCALE YOUR FIRM

When I ask our clients when they believe the right time to hire is, I usually hear two common responses. Each response is valid in its own way. The first is that it is never the right time to hire in your business. You can always say that. The second is that the right time is when you are extremely busy and need additional support.

The best answer I can give is now and always.

In working with coaching clients who desire to scale but have not done so yet, the biggest challenge is that they do not want to hire a search associate until they have enough business. There is an element of truth there, but there is never enough business, and you do not want to put a brand-new search associate on a great search. You want to put a new search associate on a nonexclusive contingency opening where you are not accountable to the client for filling the position.

You want that search associate to practice in a safe space where they can hone their skills without costing you and your firm a key account. I never put a new search associate on a retained or an exclusive search.

I give new search associates "scratch and dent" openings, where the client has full disclosure that I am using this contingency assignment to train a new recruiter. I contact a client and explain that I have a new person working on their search and assure them that any candidate they recruit will also be vetted by myself. I am using their opening as a training ground because they (the client) do not invest in retainers or believe in exclusives. Because they have been a great client in the past, I can offer our services under their terms so we can train someone on the process.

If you have the cash flow, hire in pairs. It does not take longer to train two people instead of one when you do it the right way. When it comes to hiring, pick a date, put it on a calendar, and fully commit to it. Unless there is a severe recession, it is relatively easy to go out and find a couple of scratch and dent openings for your new search associates to work on. The searches might not have the best fee or terms, but they are a great way to train a new person.

## BUILDING A CULTURE OF CONTINUOUS IMPROVEMENT

One way I built a culture of continuous improvement was through contests and incentives, which was a carrot approach to help people achieve at higher levels. Our contests and incentives were designed to give more points and value to money upfront from a client and/ or exclusive contingencies. Additionally, we provided emphasis and monitoring on week-to-week activity numbers (versus placement numbers) and the consistency of execution of their Recruiter GPS.

When these were the areas of focus that we consistently talked about in the weekly meetings as a company, we cultivated a culture of continuous improvement. When recruiters could see how they performed against what they committed to doing, they improve continuously and organically.

Another way I fostered a culture of continuous improvement was to have everyone present a professional development book each quarter to the entire office. Each team member had to read a book on motivation, technique, selling, or something that I approved that was business oriented and could help the rest of the team. The presentation included the top ten things they learned from the book and how they applied it to their work. When choosing the book, they did not have to take the rest of the office into consideration. The goal was to allow the team member to choose material intriguing to them and learn ten new concepts to apply to their practice.

## FINAL THOUGHTS

The beauty is when you learn how to scale the right way, it is the same as the other business areas we already covered. There is a system for every aspect of the process. There are specific benchmarks for search associates, account executives, and practice leaders. The specific benchmarks are how each role all tie into each other. Trying to implement this in the absence of knowing Recruiter GPS would be an exercise in futility because you are not clear how they are performing or are ready to go to the next level.

When you strictly use placements as the barometer of success, how do you know if the recruiter had a successful day or a successful week, especially when a good recruiter makes one placement per month? There are twenty-two working days in the average month. How do you know they were successful the other twenty-one?

You need Recruiter GPS to scale a business successfully and to motivate your recruiters.

# SCALABLE OPERATIONS CASE STUDY

## BILL GIBBENS – SIGHTCAST RECRUITING GROUP

Bill Gibbens is the co-founder of Sightcast Recruiting Group headquartered in Aransas Pass, Texas. He and El, his cofounder and wife, started the firm in 2005 from the ground up, specializing in permanent placement for construction, engineering, and accounting and finance industries. Bill has been a client of The RecruiterU since 2018. In 2020, in the midst of the COVID-19 pandemic, they went through a rebuilding phase that focused on hiring team members for the firm.

## WHAT IS THE USUAL CAREER PATH IN YOUR FIRM? HOW DO YOU BRING SOMEBODY IN, AND HOW DO THEY PROGRESS WITH YOU?

When we first started our firm, we brought new recruiters in as what I would call a 360-full-cycle desk mode, where we taught them everything, and on the first day on the phones, we had them marketing. And that worked – I mean, it does work. We feel like that way of onboarding is a bit more difficult, so you might have to hire a few more people to find those special ones that can handle that super-fast download of information.

About two or three years ago, we transitioned to bringing people on first as a search assistant and a recruiter. In our first couple weeks, we will show them or teach them the entire what we do – the 365 world. Still, as far as phone calls, we only have them on the phone, learning how to recruit first, getting proficient there. And then, when they are ready, they can transition to the search consultant role or more of a marketing role as well.

## HOW DO YOU DETERMINE WHO TO HIRE AND WHEN? DO YOU ALWAYS BRING THEM IN AS A SEARCH ASSOCIATE, OR DO YOU LOOK AT THE NEEDS?

You know, obviously, we're comfortable bringing people in as a 360-degree recruiter, so depending on their personality, age, income requirements, maybe a sales background, we may open that up. But as a general rule, when we are recruiting, we are first selling the search assistant position. We are now targeting people coming right out of college, relatively young. So many of my employees, we hired between the ages of twenty-one and twenty-four, which I think is fairly young for what we are doing.

The primary personality that we are looking for is somebody that is super inquisitive. If, during an interview process, it is us that is carrying the conversation, we generally do not go to the next interview. The candidate has to carry the conversation and ask a lot of questions because that is what we do. We just innately have to be obsessive about gathering information by asking relevant and smart questions. That is the primary, number one thing that we look for in prospective team members.

The other thing is stability in their life. It doesn't mean they cannot make job changes. But do they have a stable living environment, home environment – that sort of thing? Do they have a support mechanism? Because what we do is so difficult. Without that support mechanism, many will burn out.

And competitiveness – we love to see naturally competitive people. When everything else is all even, the one thing that drives us every day is our competitive nature. So, with that competitive nature, I find that it is easier to motivate and keep them engaged in times of high production or even low production. It is a key mechanism or aspect of a personality that drives a person to show up and continue bringing it.

## WHAT IS YOUR AVERAGE TENURE FOR A RECRUITER?

I have several people right now who have been with me eight years, several for four years. Our tenure is fairly good. Now, early on, our turnover was pretty high. I hired probably eighty people over a ten-year period, and I probably kept maybe four of those long-term. I am not hiring as many, but I do seem to keep them longer since, again, about three or four years ago, we transitioned in the search assistant role.

I think, again, I just predict that it's a little bit easier for people to come in. I'm still learning the transition piece – you know, when to transition them from a search assistant to a search consultant – how exactly to do that. We are still working on best practices there. I do not think it is the same for everybody. You have to look at, again, those inherent personality drivers that each person has. And there is always natural turnover – people get married and spouses move.

For the first time, COVID-19 taught us that we could work remotely, so now we have employees in San Antonio and East Texas. And going forward, at this time have shrunk our office. Now, we have an office in Aransas Pass, but I see by the end of the year, we will probably go to a bigger office, but not as large as we had pre-COVID-19. I think a lot of my workforce will be working remotely long term. So, we'll have an office more for social reasons, I think, than anything because people do want that physical connection with an office or a group of people, so I think it's important that we do that.

## DO YOU THINK THAT WILL HELP WITH RETENTION OR RECRUITING EFFORTS IN THE FUTURE WITH THE ABILITY TO WORK REMOTELY?

I am not sure about recruiting efforts. It will help with retention, and it will help with the quality of work, relationship with the people around you. We work at a virtual office every day, so we open up a Zoom office, and everybody all over Texas is Zoomed into it. It's a virtual office. We can see people. We can quickly ask questions back and forth and what have you. So, we're connected, but it's just different when you had that physical connection and you could really see somebody and work alongside them.

One of the things that I am striving to do is to keep that going by having happy hours and what have you, which has been tough because of COVID-19. Many of my employees are very concerned about catching it. We have had to be selective, but the dawn is arising now.

## HOW HAS SCALING YOUR BUSINESS IMPACTED BOTH YOUR FIRM AND YOUR PERSONAL LIFE? WHAT HAS THIS AFFORDED YOU?

Well, with the firm, it affords, I think, career paths. You are working alongside other professionals. You are bigger than something – just yourself. You have teams. We are developing business units where we can share the inventory.

A rising tide lifts all boats, so that's the theme that we're following.

Obviously, COVID-19 kind of set us back a little bit, but we are going forward with that. For us personally, in our rookie year, my wife out-billed me. She was the Rookie Billing Manager of the Year for the franchise that we were in. She would get mad because every time she would close a deal, that would give me the money to hire somebody else, so it caused a lot of friction that the first year – actually a couple of years.

You have to think about hiring as an investment in an annuity. We hired, as I mentioned, a lot of people – over eighty people in the first ten years. In the first three years, we hired twelve to fourteen people a year and maybe kept two or three. Some of these we kept for eighteen months, and some we kept for fifteen years.

But what that did for us is allow us to focus on being a coach versus a producer. We still do deals every once in a while. We still work on projects. But our business model is really not for us to produce. In fact, if I am doing deals, that probably means I'm not spending enough time with my people, coaching them, doing more deals, and making them super successful and operating at their highest level of proficiency.

So, my motivation is not to work at the desk level for me but to work and help them produce, right, at their level. It is different. That is what I get jazzed at. Again, kind of going back to my story, when I close a deal, I was not jazzed at closing a deal, and here is $30,000 or here is $40,000. It was, "Hey, that just gave me the money so I can hire another person, and I am making another deposit in my annuity."

Then, once you get tenure – once you establish that core group – it changes. And it is hard to get to that core group. It takes years and years. That is one of the issues with this business model that people probably do not understand. It takes years to really get that core tenure. Once you have it, it is like its own little asset. It is like money you can spend. "How am I going to spend that tenure?"

Your core team members can help you hire, onboard, and grow that way. You can start doing different things as far as really establishing business units. But I mean, whatever your creativity can think about and what your people can do is where you can go. I think it just opens up the world, not just for myself and my wife but also for my team.

I try to be the creator and allow them to do whatever they can do.

Having that team is different than working on a desk. Some people are jazzed at closing deals. Big billers, generally – it is all about closing the deal, and that is great. That just does not jazz me as much as motivating people.

# 12

# RECRUITER RETENTION

We have been discussing Self-Driving Business and the concepts of the Art of Delegation and Scalable Operations. Self-Driving Business is what transforms your recruiting firm from founder dependent to team run. This final chapter on Recruiter Retention is where you bring together all the pieces needed to build a real business that runs without you. Recruiter (hiring and) retention is the final piece of the puzzle that will truly liberate you in your recruiting firm.

## RECRUITER RETENTION DEFINED

The most common beliefs that I have heard that hold many recruiting firm owners back from growing their firm are that it is expensive, takes too long, or that nobody wants to work hard anymore. When I hear owners make these statements, I know that means that there are no systems, processes, or defined outcomes for hiring recruiters in their business. The reality of hiring is that if you hire 100 people, 100 people will not work out. However, if you hire 100 people the right way, most of them will, and many will be profitable even if they leave you three to six months later.

Many owners plateau in their ability to grow their firms, and when they remain plateaued, it often results in boredom or a feeling like a hamster on a treadmill. These firm owners stop intellectually stop growing into the role of the owner of a search firm. An owner of a search firm is not just a great recruiter. An owner of a search firm in a scalable operation can replicate themselves through other people.

Growth as a recruiting firm owner is what we talk about when discussing Recruiter Retention. Recruiter Retention involves attraction, selection, onboarding, training, and development. It is about creating a culture of continuous improvement and excitement for the profession of recruiting. It is about bringing out the best in your recruiters through clear expectations, accountability, and coaching.

## THE HIRING PROCESS

Hiring is where recruiting firm owners become the shoemaker's children. While we help numerous clients find great talent for their organizations each year – as the shoemaker's children have worn shoes – we often struggle to do the same for our own businesses. The reason is that most recruiting firm owners lack a standard hiring process. Full disclosure: when I started my recruiting firm, I did not have a standard hiring process. Step one is always to create a standard hiring process. This process does not have to be complicated, but it does need to be systematized.

From my own early experiences and working with clients who struggle with hiring, the first thought is that it takes a lot of time to hire. I thought, "Maybe we should post an ad or see if we can get some referrals." There was no standard process for hiring that included a finding and attraction phase, an interview process, and an offer and closing process. Creating this process means that every time you need to hire, it is done the same way every time. It means that anyone could walk into your firm and know exactly how you bring on a new team member from start to finish.

Your hiring process is part of your playbook. Each time you need to hire a new recruiter, pull out the playbook.

*Step 1: Attraction*

What is the attraction phase? Many clients have said to me that they have no idea where to find people. Post an ad on LinkedIn, a job board, a local Facebook group, or even a local newspaper's online classified section. The ad should be written not necessarily to attract someone with recruiting experience but someone looking for a career with growth opportunities., I prefer to train than re-train; therefore, I prefer to have someone without experience in recruiting.

Attraction is not just posting an ad; that is not always going to work. What works even better than a great job posting is an excellent employee referral program. Ask them to share your posting on their social media and LinkedIn pages. Incentivize your employees to bring great talent to you to interview.

*Step 2: Recruiting*

Having a recruiting process means you will go out and do for yourself what you do for your clients. We contact companies like ADP, Paychex, or local computer service companies in my recruiting firm. I search for people with series six or seven certifications, which is public information, especially for people earlier in their careers. These people are struggling because building up a thriving financial services practice takes a long time. I look for people who were selling commodity-based products.

From there, either you or someone in your firm who has recruiting internal talent as part of their role should reach out to these people to have a recruiting conversation. These passive candidates become the basis of your talent pool. Posting an ad, getting employee referrals, and doing active recruiting are three examples; when done together, they give you a consistent flow of candidates and a big enough pool to pick from.

### *Step 3: Interviewing*

Once you complete the attraction and recruiting steps, you move onto the interview process. Again, this process should be the same each time you interview candidates. A great interview process includes a plan for the first interview, the second interview, and the offer.

The first interview was always on the phone with me. These interviews were with candidates replying to the ad or people we recruited. My first question to each person was always, "Why are you interested in the recruiting position?"

If I liked what the candidate had to say on that call, the candidate moved onto a face-to-face interview. We had a plan for the second interview. If the face-to-face interview went well, the candidate then moved onto the final step.

The final interview was meeting with somebody on our team. I relied on my team member to ask similar questions that I asked in the phone and face-to-face interviews and a few others that uncovered anything the candidate neglected to share. The team member also listened for language or questions that indicated that this person would or would not be an excellent fit for the office. If I could get a signal from my team member during this final interview, I extended an offer to the candidate at the end of this interview.

### *Step 4: Offer and Closing*

The final step of the process is the offer and closing, which is where I see our coaching clients stumble. You are a recruiter. You know people can make counteroffers. You know people can make competing offers. It happens with your clients, and it will happen to you if you do not have a firm offer and closing process.

Do you have a process in place to close the candidate? By process, I mean, do you get their commitment? Whenever I came to the offer stage with a candidate, the conversation was always, "I am going to make you an offer. If you say yes, I want that yes to be a commitment because I am going to release the backup candidates for this role. You are going to start two weeks from today. I will put together a written offer. Do I have your commitment?" If this conversation sounds familiar, that is because it is the same conversation I have with a candidate on a search.

The interview process has concrete steps. The beauty of these specific steps is it creates a system that you can calendar. This systemized process allows you to plan your entire process all the way through training and onboarding. Growing your team then becomes a project that you can integrate into your daily, weekly, monthly, and quarterly plan. When you can plan it, you control it instead of the hiring process controlling you.

## TRAINING AND ONBOARDING

Having a systemized, repeatable process for hiring is a big part of Recruiter Retention. However, for many recruiting firm owners, the entire process falls apart is at the point of onboarding. What are the qualities of a great new recruiter onboarding program to make sure that this new hire sticks?

Onboarding is where most recruiting firm owners develop a belief of "I can't find anyone willing to work hard." They are the ones who are inadvertently creating this scenario by having their new hire watch a training or do specific tasks. Still, these activities are rarely any specifics behind exactly what will be covered or when it will be covered, or they are not bound by timeframes.

Most training programs fail because they are rarely developed with both the outcome and timeframe in mind. Determine the outcome that you want from an onboarding program and the specific period in which to achieve that outcome.

In my firm – and I recommend this to our clients who own recruiting firms – we create an overall defined outcome for the first two months. From that overarching outcome, we reverse engineer specific outcomes for the first two months, first month, first two weeks, first week, and first day. By engaging in this process of developing your onboarding program, you ensure that you are beginning with the result. The eventual outcome drives each step toward the desired outcome rather than planning each step in hopes of achieving it. It may sound counterintuitive, but it a proven practice in training and professional development.

In my firm, the content portion of our training program was a day and a half. On the afternoon of day two, new recruiters were put on the phone with a precise objective. Day three consisted of heavy phone work with a clear expectation of exactly how many people they would talk to. For us, it was fifteen live conversations.

Every time I explain the onboarding cadence and fifteen-conversation minimum to new clients or at live events, at least one person argues that in the 2020s, that is impossible. No, full stop. We have several clients onboarding new hires using this method and standard today. For new recruiters to successfully do that, there has to be an excellent plan in place for them. They will need an extensive list of names to call and guidance on how to begin the conversation.

The goal of fifteen conversations per day starting on day three serves several purposes. By having fifteen conversations per day, your new recruiter will not perfect their presentation skills in three days. Those conversations will be highly imperfect – so cringeworthy that I do not recommend that you listen to the call recordings the first day or two. The ultimate goal is to compact all the failures as quickly as possible to give them a feeling for the business.

Remember, you are defining the outcomes and asking yourself, "What do I want?"

The expectation for the first whole week on a desk is to have the new recruiter speak to seventy-five people. I recommend listening to their call recordings and, each day, sitting down with them for a half-hour to forty-five minutes to review their calls and give them feedback. During this onboarding stage, the recruiter will have a consistent expectation of fifteen conversations every day, which is a non-negotiable daily goal for setting up the accountability relationship between you and your team.

Remember, you will be designing an overall onboarding program with clear outcomes and expectations at each point of the new recruiter's career development. The following stages require a quality search assignment at the end of two months, an exclusive, or maybe even money upfront. At the end of thirty days, their role may be to find and develop talent. Benchmarks along the way may include asking, "Can they take a quality datasheet?" based on your firm's definition of a quality datasheet. I could always identify a motive for making a career change and clearly match the candidate's skillset with the assignment. These are just a few examples; your outcomes and expectations may be different based on the roles of the recruiters you are hiring.

Determining specific outcomes and setting clear expectations is only half of the battle. I see many people fail despite having clear outcomes and expectations because they do not set specific accountabilities in the training program for activity – or, if they do, they do not have accountability or a consequence process.

### *Accountability*

Accountability is the not-so-secret to success for any training and onboarding program. While clear outcomes, expectations, and an execution plan are essential, holding your new hires and tenured recruiters accountable is the secret to success. Accountability is what allows your team to stay on track and grow within their role. It is also what allows you, as the firm owner, to assess what support a team member may need to be successful each step of the way. If people are not clear on what they are accountable for, and you are not clear, you do not know if it is a skill issue or a motivation issue.

Accountability, especially in the first weeks of a new hire's tenure, was crucial. For us, if somebody made less than fifteen conversations per day, I gave them a warning. After one or two warnings, they were terminated. When I say this to coaching clients and at seminars, many people say that is brutal. The reality is, I only fired two or three people in the first few weeks. People get the message quickly when you set accountability the right way. A successful onboarding program has specific timeframes, outcomes, and schedule for when you will do certain things.

One of the things that I did wrong for a long time was having the typical owner complaint of "people don't want to work." "I don't understand why they won't just…" In the early to mid-1990s, I reflected on my turnover rates and studied why some recruiters were successful and others were not.

I quickly realized that I was missing accountability. We were tracking metrics, but I was not using the metrics to their best ability. I went back and looked at how many people I hired versus how many people made it up to that point. The results were one out of twenty were successful despite my inadequate training and development, which means that these new hires had all the internal dials filled in, and they were going to succeed in spite of me.

When I talked to other owners, people left to their own devices and motivation have a 5 percent success rate, which does not mean only one in twenty will make it as a recruiter. What it means is that one in twenty was wildly successful without accountability. When I added accountability (which reduced how many recruiters I needed to hire), three out of five were wildly successful, and the other two were just okay. Integrating accountability completely changed the number. I realized thousands of percentage points of improvement by simply running the same training program and combining it with accountability.

## MOTIVATING YOUR TEAM

Training, onboarding, and accountability are what get your new recruiters going. Motivation is what keeps your entire office energized. How do you motivate your team?

Once a new hire is up and running, there will come a point in time when they get bored. Think about it: If you are a tenured owner, there comes a time when you get bored with the things you do in the business. There are elements in every role where the challenge disappears after doing the same thing repeatedly. What may have been challenging a year or two ago isn't anymore.

If this is not addressed correctly, a big billing tenured person may want to go off on their own because they think if they are on their own, there will be a more significant challenge, they can make more money by themselves, et cetera.

I always thought of myself – and you can too – as the owner who needed to be version two, three, or four of my team members. Even when I took myself off a desk, I never stopped studying marketing and selling. I was consistently striving to add more value to my recruiters so they knew working for me allowed them to close more business than they could on their own.

Then, there comes a time – generally around when a recruiter hits about a quarter of a million dollars in annual billings – where you can leverage their desk. By leverage, I mean you hire somebody to develop candidates for their searches, which is the search associate role. That big biller then transitions into a team leader. Once you build a team underneath a big biller, you significantly increase the likelihood they stay with you long term. I never lost a team leader. In fact, my team leaders are the people who bought out my company.

Motivate your recruiters by raising their level of challenge constantly. Just like you got tired of taking datasheets, most of them will get tired of taking datasheets on candidates. Even though they won't ever stop doing this task, their roles will shift. Change the focus to getting more assignments at a higher level, which is a task that they are good at, and developing this other person on their team.

Developing people into leaders on their own teams is powerful for building your business, and recognizing performance is essential to Recruiter Retention. In addition to creating new growth opportunities, invest in training; send your people to conferences, virtual or in-person; and run contests.

### *Incentives and Contests as a Retention Strategy*

A rule of thumb is to invest 2 to 3 percent of your gross revenue into incentives and contests. These can be things such as a rewards trip if they hit a certain level of billings or a President's-Club-type trip where you take them to someplace like Hawaii, the Caribbean, or a resort for three or four days. We ran several contests that rewarded activities that led to placements, job orders, or first-time interviews. We created points for the specific aspect we were measuring and tailored incentives around that. Combining that with constant career growth was one of the few of the ways I keep my team motivated.

While working toward an annual trip is a great motivator, another successful motivation strategy is shorter sprint-type contests. These contests can have the most precious reward of all, time off. In my experience, extra time is the most significant and most precious asset that you can be granted. Since recruiting is such a metrics-driven environment, you can adjust the activity on your desk to grant yourself time off if you are a solo or allow your recruiters to earn extra time off.

When your financial goals are being met, the biggest motivator is not more money but more time. In the recruiting industry, the week between Christmas and New Year's and the week around the Fourth of July are two weeks of each year when the industry slows down. I always take those weeks as a vacation. However, I did not give these weeks off *carte blanche* to the team; I made them earn it.

One of the time-off-type contests we ran was called "Five in Four." This is just one example of many contents you can implement in your recruiting firm. Most years, there are four full weeks between Thanksgiving and Christmas. If you are in Europe or another part of the world where you do not have Thanksgiving, you can use the four full weeks before Christmas. Christmas week is a slow week around the globe, but you can use whatever national holiday is best in your region of the world.

The contest was accomplishing what your goals were for five weeks in four weeks and get the week between Christmas and New Year's off. We did the same content terms between Memorial Day and Fourth of July, which is usually about four weeks. Accomplish five weeks of productivity in four weeks, and you get the week of Fourth of July off.

Note that the contest is about productivity, not placements. Placements are always a lagging indicator of activity. If the individual recruiter's goal is two first-time interviews a week because two interviews a week get them $300,000 a year in billings, they need to arrange ten interviews in four weeks, and they get the fifth week off.

You can also do creative things. For example, in the

summer, let your recruiters earn Friday off by hitting their activity goal on Thursday. These are little things that will drive up productivity into sprints. Once someone works at a sprint, they usually do not revert to their previous activity level. When it drops back down, it never goes back down to the baseline. They may not stay at this higher level, but you are always creating incremental increases. Each time you do these types of contests, you are leveling up your team's productivity.

## FINAL THOUGHTS

I forgot who I heard this from because I would love to give them credit; as an owner when you get to a real business where you are scaling, and there came the point when I took myself off a desk, a lot of times, people wonder: "What is a great day? What does a great week look like for me as an owner in this role?"

It really frames around what Jeff Kaye of Kaye/Bassman International said to me: "Now that I do not have clients anymore, I mean our company has clients, but now that I do not have individual clients anymore because I am off a desk, my clients are my team. My job then is to grow that client base, meaning add more people, and retain that client base." It was just a phenomenal metaphor. Think of your team members as clients. What do you need to do to serve them at a high level to raise their performance, keep them happy, and help them enjoy coming to work? Then, expand that "client base" with other team members.

The main reason I see people not hiring is because they believe people do not want to work hard, hiring is expensive, and that hiring takes too much time. None of those beliefs are true. Yes, you need to invest in ninety to 120 days in a new person. Structured this the right way, this is thirty only to forty-five minutes per day!

In my firm, the revenue from a new person is not going to come in for four months. That is an investment. But if somebody worked on my desk – meaning they sourced candidates on my desk – a $1 investment brought me back about $3 in profitability. How is that expensive? That even considers those I hired that failed! Not 100 percent of the people you are going to hire are successful.

The lack of a structured onboarding program is why it takes too much time for so many recruiting firm owners. A structured onboarding program includes videos that can teach the content and defined coaching times with you each day. During the first week, I dedicated ninety minutes a day to coaching and training a new hire. Beginning in week two and through the second month, I reduced the coaching time to forty-five minutes a day.

This structure was the entire onboarding program. When I ask you if you could hire an onboard a new recruiter in forty-five minutes a day, could you do it? Many say they absolutely would. The reason owners think training a new recruiter takes all day is because there is no structure around it. Once you have structure around it, it does not take that long.

Finally, accountability is the cure for not being able to find people who want to work hard. I always ask somebody who mentions that as a concern, "What is your accountability process? What is your onboarding program as it is defined?" Almost 100 percent of the time, they have no accountability process or no defined onboarding program. Their onboarding program says that if you work hard and do all the right things, you will make a lot of money. That is a fluff promise without a concrete foundation.

Define your outcomes and expectations for success, and

then hold your new and tenured recruiters accountable. Invest in their ongoing development and learning. Create incentives and contests to keep everyone motivated and engaged. These three activities will help you grow your recruiting firm and create a Self-Driving Business.

# RECRUITER RETENTION CASE STUDY

## DION BOWDEN – SEARCHRSA

Dion Bowden is the founder of Searchrsa based in Johannesburg, South Africa, and Atlanta, Georgia. Since 2001, Searchrsa has provided recruiting and staffing services to the actuarial, finance, chemical, mining, and manufacturing industries. Dion has also been a client of The RecruiterU since 2009 and is a coach in our Platinum and Boardroom programs.

## WHAT BEST PRACTICES DID YOU IMPLEMENT FOR ONBOARDING NEW RECRUITERS IN YOUR FIRM?

The term "onboarding a new recruiter" begins right at the first outreach to them as an employee for your firm – that setting of expectations and deliverables and how you present the job of a recruiter to them. The first part of onboarding is making sure that you explain that this is an activity-based business when you are reaching out to them. There are certain things that they need to do on a daily basis in order to achieve their revenue goals, and if they do those activities, they will be successful.

Set those expectations from the first interview; put that through the first interview to the second interview to the third final, closing interview; and make sure you are always repeating that message.

When they come on the first day, we ensure that we are now enforcing those expectations with how they behave. So, we explain that the most important thing we do as recruiters is get candidates and clients in front of each other. In order to do that, we need to be speaking to clients, and we need to speak to candidates. So, we get them focused on that very early on, and make sure that we are setting them up for success. If that does not work for them, then we would want to fail them quickly so that they go on to better things for themselves. But if they follow that process – and it starts right at the beginning with our initial advert and throughout our initial first few days and weeks with them – we maximize the probability that they will succeed.

The second thing that we do is to break the role down into manageable chunks.

We do not put them on a desk and expect them to be 360-full-cycle recruiters. We bring them and give them a specific outcome that we require from them initially, and that outcome we have taught them to do is what they can reasonably handle with minimum training and development. We do not want to bring them on and try to get them to do everything in the recruiting business. If we start them as a recruiting coordinator, they are just reaching out to candidates and having an initial screening conversation with them. Or they are doing marketing presentations if they come from a business development environment and are doing some initial "flip" marketing calls or MPC marketing campaigns. But they are handing it over to somebody senior.

Two things: one is to set the expectations of deliverables, and then the second part is to make sure that we are not giving them too much – that we set them up to give them a task that they will most likely be successful at because it is such a well-defined event.

## WHAT DO YOU FEEL THE ROLE OF ACCOUNTABILITY HAS ON RECRUITER RETENTION?

Accountability has everything to do with retention for a recruiter because proper accountability means that they will hit their goals. Accountability means they are accountable to themselves, not necessarily to you as the recruiting firm owner. You would sit in conjunction with them and make goals for the year. You would ask their permission to hold them accountable to their own goals, not your goals. Because their goals inevitably are far in excess of what you need as a firm owner from your recruiter. Their goals can be broken down scientifically to the month, week, and day activity-wise using metrics or Recruiter GPS, so there is no mystery in them hitting their billing goal!

You would ask them to give you permission to hold them

accountable to their own goals. So, you hold them accountable to themselves. As the firm owner, you are merely the mirror and showing back at them what they set for themselves.

Once you do that, then alongside planning and removing the anxiety as a firm owner, so that removes anxiety as a firm owner, and really what you are now becoming is a coach who gets your team member to where they want to be in their career. So, the accountability, at the end of the day, is to themselves.

# 13

# WHY YOU WON'T IMPLEMENT WHAT YOU LEARNED

Most people who read this book won't implement a single strategy. Some will implement a couple, struggle a little, and revert to their old habits. A small fraction will implement a few ideas and get great results but ignore the other ideas. Why?

For years, The RecruiterU coached and trained people to achieve exactly what they said they wanted for themselves and their business. We walked clients through, step by step, exactly what had to be done. All of them got excited to have a custom-designed road map leading to what they truly desired in their business.

Some clients executed brilliantly and doubled, tripled, and decupled their business revenue without working longer or harder. On the other hand, some clients procrastinated. Some froze from fear. A small percent even stopped mid program. All were exposed to the same content and the same processes. There was no mystery as to what the next steps were for them.

I asked myself, "Why is Mary getting great results while Joe is struggling?" My old response was to fine tune the technique or deepen the strategy. That rarely helped. Over time I discovered the reason why some of our clients were doing significantly better than others was very simple: *mindset*.

When I say mindset, I mean a person's thoughts and beliefs. But not their thoughts and beliefs to do things, like implement the changes in this book. I'm talking about their thoughts and beliefs *about* things: different mindsets about money and desire, discipline and time management, and trust and fear.

Unlike most professionals, recruiters have wildly different thought and beliefs about themselves and their business, and they make a huge impact on the recruiter's ability to take risks, make changes, and meet their full potential even with a rock-solid strategy. And since you invested your time reading this book, I want to cover a few areas that will help you execute with an Elite Recruiter's Mindset!

The first mindset gap between recruiters who implement on things in this book and those that won't are differences in their beliefs and thoughts around desire. If you want to be part of the small fraction that gets sustainable results, start with a clear, written vision. You need a clear vision of what you truly want and desire in both your business and your life. Why? Your brain works off *images*. "$200,000 more in billing" is *not* an image. What will that $200,000 provide you that resonates with true desire? Is it

- Financial security? Then imagine being truly financially secure. What does that look like and feel like?

- Paying off all debt? Then imagine being debt free. How are you different?

- A down payment toward an amazing vacation home? Then,

where is it? What does it look like *exactly*? Is it by an ocean or lake or in the woods? What are you doing there?

- Freedom? Then define this in pictures, images, and experiences. What does freedom mean to you, exactly?

The study conducted by Aaron Berkowitz and David Ansari that was described in Chapter 4 proved that your brain does *not* know the difference between what you think you experienced and what you actually experienced! Once you imagine and build images of something you truly desire, your brain will reveal the first steps to achieving it.

You have goals and desires for your business and life. Are they specific? Do they come from a place of *true* desire or what you think you *should* want for yourself?

Let us assume for the moment it is a pure desire that you want. Make those results appear in your life. As soon as you decide you want to have something in your life, your subconscious will give you reasons why you can't have them or shouldn't have them. This is where fear doubt and worry creep in.

Recruiters have completely different thoughts and beliefs about fear. As a result, they would allow fear to drive them into action or stop them dead in their tracks, especially in areas like marketing, hiring for their team, or asking for retainers.

For instance, I taught *exactly* how to get a deposit on a search to two different *client* recruiters. Both *clients* declared they wanted to do this to have better clients on better terms, so the desire was there. One went out and got a deposit within a week. The other did not even try to execute the process. When I asked both, "What happened?" the one who got the deposit talked about how they felt the fear of changing their approach. They confessed that in the moment, they felt fear about potentially losing the assignment – that they might "mess up" how they executed the process, that they wouldn't be perfect, et cetera – but did it anyway!

The recruiters who do not execute often have thoughts and beliefs about themselves that let fear win. They struggle with it and try their best to work through it, but ultimately, they procrastinate. They freeze. They stay stuck. The ones who froze felt the same fear as the ones who got the deposit and did the work with the fear present. The ones who froze and procrastinated allowed their fear to win.

Most people expect to find a way to do something they have never done before or to stretch themselves into new areas and challenges without fear! They wait for fear to magically disappear before they take action. I have never seen this happen. If you are going to do something you have never done before, isn't it natural to experience fear? If you don't experience fear entering the unknown, you are either a sociopath or the challenge isn't a significant enough challenge. Believe me, changing your recruiting strategies is a significant challenge.

Fortunately, we now recognize this and have a tremendous coaching process to help our clients work through their fears. We help them see the real truth in the situation beyond the fear. The results they get because they stepped into the fear with the right coaching are rewarding to us. Simply changing the way you think about a situation can have remarkable differences in your ability to implement those ideas successfully.

Once you are clear on your desired outcome and are ready to execute with "fear" present, there is one more reason you might stop. You might mistakenly think you need to know all of the steps to getting you where you want to go. That is not true.

What you need to know is what you want. The desire

needs to be specific; it needs to inspire you. You might get overwhelmed with all of the steps you must take to get you where you want to go

I cannot tell you how many recruiters I've met who have the desire and a willingness to take risks but get so stressed out by the crushing weight of their own to-do list that they can't imagine having the time to work on their busines. They, too, stay stuck. But the belief that you have to know all the steps, and you have to get it all done, just is not true. You only need to know the first step. That's it.

Next, decide to have it!

- If you decide and quit because it's hard, you will not get it

- If you decide and quit because it's not comfortable, you will not get it

- If you decide it takes too much time, you will not get it

- If you decide it's too expensive, you will not achieve it

Deciding means unrelenting execution through difficulty and fear! You only need to know the first step. That's it. After you begin executing the first step, the second step will reveal itself to you. It may not be the step you want to take – it may be a difficult step – but it will always reveal itself.

Imagine you are going to drive from New York City to Los Angeles and start the journey after dark. You program your GPS and turn on your headlights. You don't memorize the map or try to see beyond the 100 meters or so your headlights provide. You follow the route. Each turn reveals itself in the GPS after you travel the previous distance. After every meter you drive, your headlights reveal another meter of road. After days and hours of faithfully following your GPS and your headlights, you arrive in Los Angeles. You may have blown a tire. You might have missed a few turns. You might have been detoured. But you stuck to the journey. You made it!

A clear, written vision is your destination. Metrics are your GPS. The engine that runs your business vehicle are the integrated systems in this book. The fuel to move forward is becoming a preferred partner and delegating sourcing, recruiting, administration, et cetera.

What you want is here for you to take. Will you be comfortable being uncomfortable to build a business that can run without you? Or will you stay in the "story" of how hard it is, how recruiters don't want to work hard, how clients low ball fees, how candidates are liars, et cetera?

You – and only you – have the power to decide. An absence of a decision is also a decision. It is a decision to settle and stay the same.

What do you decide about your business twelve months from now? Take a minute and write it down right:

> "I, [name], decide that this will be true in my recruiting firm twelve months from [today's date]: ..."

# 14

# CREATING A REAL RECRUITING BUSINESS

This book is based on The RecruiterU's Recruiting Firm Optimizer Model. I use this model as a self-assessment at every event and with client to create awareness and improvement opportunities on the path to creating a real business that has Predictable Profits, Reliable Growth and Business Freedom. The beauty of this model is its simplicity.

Creating Predictable Profits required Clarity of Vision that build around images. Next, you can make your dreams a reality by calculating the metrics required to achieve your revenue goals. Once you know what your daily and weekly active targets are, you can create a focused plan to achieve those targets. Together, these three elements will take you from roller revenue to steady income, creating Certain Revenue on your desk and in your recruiting firm.

The next element of a real recruiting business is becoming a Pursued Partner. So many recruiters are treated like annoying vendors because of how they approach the business. Becoming a trusted advisor is all about how you approach New Client Development. Recruiters who ask consultative questions tend to have more success and better relationships with clients and prospects. Having a Powerful Presentation will allow you to land better searches, better fees, and set you up for successful landing retained, deposit-based, or exclusive assignments. The final step to becoming a Pursued Partner is flawlessly executing on the search. This means you are able to find passive talent, successfully negotiate the offer process, and make sure that the candidate your client wants to hire is ready to accept the offer with the being tempted by a counteroffer.

To create Business Freedom, you need to create a Self-Driving Business. Regardless of the size of your recruiting firm, mastering the Art of Delegation is key if you are going to achieve Business Freedom. So many clients say that they became entrepreneurs because they wanted freedom, but they hold tight onto tasks like invoicing, database management, and sourcing, all of which that can easily handed off to someone else. Delegation is the first step to Scalable Operations. Once you see how allowing others to do parts of your job, you will notice how growing your team creates leverage in your recruiting firm. I outline the different roles recruiters can play in your business and how to get started. Finally, once you build a team, you will want to retain the best and release those who are not meeting expectations quickly. When you have a system in place for hiring and training, growing and retaining great recruiters doubles your revenue without doubling your effort or time.

In all, this book provides a system to create an impact in all nine of these areas of your recruiting firm. You will find that mastery of each area is possible, but as you grow, you will have challenges come up that will require you to go back and focus on that specific area of the business. Your vision may change as your grow, or your metrics may change with the addition of a new desk specialty. Regardless, this book will give you the foundation to build your real recruiting business.

# ACKNOWLEDGMENTS

I am extremely humbled by and grateful for everyone who made this book actually come to fruition. It is a culmination of information acquired over the past thirty-plus years in the field of recruiting, millions of dollars in mistakes, and the learning from those mistakes.

A very special thank you goes to Tinamarie Berger, our director of client journey and one of our coaches. She was the first full-time member of The RecruiterU back in 2013, responsible for reigning me in. She is part of the foundation of The RecruiterU and a huge part of our company's success. Additionally, despite my procrastination, doubts, other "shiny objects," et cetera, she has persisted in keeping this book project on target. Her masterful editing, wonderful ideas, and interviews for our client case studies added significantly to the success of the finished product. By the time is published, she should be Dr. Tinamarie Berger with a doctor of education degree in organizational change and leadership.

Thanks also to my masterful lead coaches Kathleen Kurke and Dion Bowden. Both kick me in the butt continuously to push me out of my comfort zone. Thanks to Kathleen for driving the operational side of The RecruiterU and to Dion for pushing me to create my first groups and 7-Figure Boardroom Owner Mastermind.

Thanks to our lead mindset coach, Frances Walker, who brought the invaluable dimension of helping our clients get out of their own way and have the things in their business they truly desired after years of being "stuck."

To the rest of our coaching team – Ardith Rademacher, Pam Winholtz, Bill Gibbens, Beth Todd, Grant Porteous, and Kaito Bangudi – who have all proven that I don't need to be the "coach" to our clients and that when you surround yourselves with amazing coaches, your clients will get amazing results.

To Lydia Walter, our chief marketing officer. Her marketing may be the reason you are reading this book! Her teamwork with Priscilla Hoover ensures we bring in clients who we can help and who are open to coaching, change, and reaching levels in their recruiting business previously thought of as unrealistic.

To our support team of Nancy Walter and Saralyn Savage for keeping the "trains running on time" at The RecruiterU.

A big thanks also to The Author Incubator, who helped us navigate the final leg of this publishing process, from naming the book to organizing it in such a way to have the most impact on you, the reader. My old friend and founder Angela Lauria jumped in and offered so much valuable help, we hired them to complete the project. Thanks also to Trever McKenzie, whose detailed reviews made the work even better!

A special thanks to all my mentors. They *all* pushed, challenged, annoyed, and cajoled me to be both a better human being and a better, more profitable business owner. Pasquale Scopelliti was the first coach I ever hired. I remember thinking how expensive he was back in the mid-nineties when I engaged him initially. Our work together over a decade is, to this day, the *best* investment I have ever made in myself. Thank *you*, Pasquale, for seeing a "bigger" me than I saw in myself. Thank you for pushing me on my metrics and their importance.

To my other mentors, Kevin Nations, Taki Moore, David Neagle, Dan Sullivan, and Craig Filek. This journey is too hard to do alone. Thanks to all of you for seeing my blind spots, not buying my bullshit, and pushing me to be "comfortable being uncomfortable."

A special thanks to my wife of over thirty years, Tracey Gionta, for supporting me in starting a business when we first got married, having no idea if we would succeed but having the faith that we would. Also, to my three children, Meghan, Amy, and Christopher. You were always my inspiration to build a business that would run without me there so I could be present watching you grow up.

Thank you to my mom, who had to raise three kids by herself after my dad passed when I was six years old. Thank you for all the sacrifices you made that have allowed me to become the person I am today.

Thanks to all my friends and relatives who ground me and keep me real. There are too many to mention without accidentally leaving some out. I am truly blessed with an amazing circle of supportive humans in my life.

Last but not least, a special thank you to all of our clients who push themselves past their fears into their zone of genius, building the business they always wanted but doubted was possible. It is you who inspire not only me but our entire team to push the envelope on strategies, mindset, techniques, et cetera for you to achieve even more exceptional levels in both your personal and professional lives.

# ABOUT THE AUTHOR

Mike is one of the most recognized names in the recruiting industry today. After almost going out of business in 1991, Mike used his numerous "learning experiences" to build his personal billings to more than one million dollars per year consistently, with his best year in personal billings of $2,143,000. His recruiting firm, The Hudson Consulting Group, was rated the eleventh fastest-growing technology search firm in the U.S. and the second largest recruiting agency in the greater Hartford area.

Mike then founded TheRecruiterU.com in 2007, and he and his associate coaches have helped solo and independent recruiting firm owners get better clients, scale their business, and finally create Business Freedom. The RecruiterU mentors clients on how to use Mike's tested and proven strategies to multiply their earnings without working longer, harder hours. His training and coaching on becoming a trusted advisor and getting deposit-based searches transformed the way recruiters conduct their business. Additionally, Mike's systems for hiring and onboarding new recruiters revolutionized how recruiting agencies scale their operations.

Recognizing that many of the reasons recruiting firm owners are stuck, bored, and frustrated with their business is simply how they *think* about their business, he led The RecruiterU to be the industry's first coaching/ training organization to incorporate mindset/ performance coaching alongside business strategy coaching.

Mike also authored *How To Double Your Placements in 121 Days or Less* and is published frequently in leading recruiting industry trade journals. In addition, Mike is a keynote speaker at Recruiting Franchise Organizations and the National and State Recruiting Conferences.

Because Mike has built two businesses that run without him there, he has been active coaching high school baseball, is the president of his local Little League, sits on local boards, takes commissions, and serves as a campaign manager in his local elections.

**Website:** https://therecruiteru.com

**Facebook:** https://www.facebook.com/therecruiteru

**Email:** mikeg@therecruiteru.com

# ABOUT DIFFERENCE PRESS

DIFFERENCE
PRESS

Difference Press is the exclusive publishing arm of The Author Incubator, an educational company for entrepreneurs – including life coaches, healers, consultants, and community leaders – looking for a comprehensive solution to get their books written, published, and promoted. Its founder, Dr. Angela Lauria, has been bringing to life the literary ventures of hundreds of authors-in-transformation since 1994.

A boutique-style self-publishing service for clients of The Author Incubator, Difference Press boasts a fair and easy-to-understand profit structure, low-priced author copies, and author-friendly contract terms. Most importantly, all of our #incubatedauthors maintain ownership of their copyright at all times.

## LET'S START A MOVEMENT WITH YOUR MESSAGE

In a market where hundreds of thousands of books are published every year and are never heard from again, The Author Incubator is different. Not only do all Difference

Press books reach Amazon bestseller status, but all of our authors are actively changing lives and making a difference.

Since launching in 2013, we've served over 500 authors who came to us with an idea for a book and were able to write it and get it self-published in less than 6 months. In addition, more than 100 of those books were picked up by traditional publishers and are now available in bookstores. We do this by selecting the highest quality and highest potential applicants for our future programs.

Our program doesn't only teach you how to write a book – our team of coaches, developmental editors, copy editors, art directors, and marketing experts incubate you from having a book idea to being a published, bestselling author, ensuring that the book you create can actually make a difference in the world. Then we give you the training you need to use your book to make the difference in the world, or to create a business out of serving your readers.

## ARE YOU READY TO MAKE A DIFFERENCE?

You've seen other people make a difference with a book. Now it's your turn. If you are ready to stop watching and start taking massive action, go to http://theauthorincubator.com/apply/.

"Yes, I'm ready!"

# OTHER BOOKS BY DIFFERENCE PRESS

*The Scholarship Playbook for Parents of Student-Athletes: Stop Fouling Out and Start Scoring Money for College* by Dr. Simoné Edwards

*When Marriage Needs a Miracle: The Modern Woman's Guide to Figure out the Future of Your Relationship* by Shari Kubinec

*Conquer the Classroom: How to Manage Your Students, Your Administration, and Yourself* by Robin Reed Riggle, B.F.A., M.Ed.

# THANK YOU

Congratulations! You've taken the first step! You are on your way!

The easiest way for me to stay true to my desire and achieve it quicker than I thought possible was to be exposed to world class mentors. I was truly blessed to meet some of the finest out there. I was blessed with success that came from having great teams and great coaches/ mentors.

I remember seeing Michael Jordan and Tiger Woods, arguably two of the greatest in their sports at their peak, talk about the value of having someone watch their shots to see what they could not see. They shared how much it helped improve their performance.

I remember thinking that if greats like Jordan and Woods had coaches, I could benefit greatly from one, too. My coaches and mentors saw my blindsides. They saw completely different ways of thinking and different paths for me to achieve my desired outcome. They saved/ made me millions I could not have on my own. If I did it, would have taken years longer to get there.

The RecruiterU has helped hundreds of recruiting firm

owners get more and better clients on great terms. We helped owners hire recruiters in ways that make them productive quickly without micromanaging them. We helped them make their business fun again while working fewer hours. If you would like to see if or how we can help you get similar results, email me at MikeG@theRecruiterU.com for a complimentary consultation.

To access templates to help you excel in each of the nine areas of the Recruiting Firm Optimizer Model, visit www.therecruiteru.com/book.

# FREE RESOURCES

To access some of the templates outlined in this book go to:

**www.TheRecruiterU.com/book**

Printed in Great Britain
by Amazon

38843729R00126